Openness Mind

Openness
Mind

Tarthang Tulku

DHARMA PUBLISHING

NYINGMA PSYCHOLOGY SERIES

1. *Reflections of Mind*
2. *Gesture of Balance*
3. *Openness Mind*
4. *Kum Nye Relaxation*
5. *Skillful Means*
6. *Hidden Mind of Freedom*
7. *Knowledge of Freedom: Time to Change*

LIBRARY OF CONGRESS CATALOGING IN PUBLICATION DATA

Tarthang Tulku.
    Openness mind.

    (Nyingma psychology series; 3)
    1. Meditation (Lamaism)—Addresses, essays, lectures.
I. Title.
BQ7805.T37   294.3'4'43   78-13659
ISBN 0-913546-55-0
ISBN 0-913546-56-9 pbk.

Frontispiece: Tara

Editing, Illustration, and Design by Dharma Publishing
Typeset in Fototronic Continental and Illumna
Printed and bound by Dharma Press

9

Contents

*Dedicated to Western
students of the Dharma*

Foreword

Many books talk about Buddhism, but few communicate its meaning. In order to awaken understanding in others, one has first to know and then to live what one knows. Knowledge so lived is communicated effortlessly as part of an endlessly creative process.

Openness Mind is a book through which Buddhism speaks to the reader. Its opening chapter already emphasizes the importance of learning—not so much as an accumulation of data (although the accumulation of data is obviously indispensable for the learning process), but rather as an endeavor to understand. But how are we to understand unless we return to the source from which we have abstracted the data? The source is experience—experience before it is channeled through the familiar pattern of ordinary thinking which turns everything into something quantifiable and measurable, in brief, into isolated, lifeless data—taking the qualitative out of life.

The return to experience which insists on the qualitative as integral to life needs another kind of thinking. Whether 'meditation' is, under present circumstances, still the appropriate term for it, is, of course, debatable. The term has been overused and, in popular parlance, has acquired too much of an esoteric or mystical-mystifying nimbus, while its intention is the very opposite. Meditation is, first of all, a process of learning, of intent concentration on an object or a situation in order to gain insight into its unique nature so as to be able to cope efficiently with it. We, as living beings, are always in a situation, not so much in the sense of being an isolated entity in a container, with both 'entities' having no relation to each other, but rather as of being spread throughout the situation. In other words, through intent concentration on an object or situation, we learn to discern and to appreciate the possibilities of a situation.

On the basis of this awareness we then learn to act in an appropriate manner, which means not to do violence to the delicate fabric of a life situation. In this sense 'meditation' is a way of experiencing, quite concretely, any situation in which we may find ourselves. It is in no way something transcendental or 'abstract', but is eminently 'practical' in aiding us to become alive again by restoring the free flow of life's stream. In Buddhism, 'meditation', as should be clear by now, is not a running away from thinking, but is the applicability and application of this kind of 'thinking' in daily life. That is the leitmotif of this book.

To the extent that the reader is drawn into what may be termed 'applied Buddhism', the reader will note that the book, in its progression from chapter to chapter, is a 'trail guide'. The field through which it points the way is the rich and intricate nature of man. In thus being a guide, the book is very traditional in the sense that it restates the fact that man is capable of growth and that growth is a continuous process of expansion into ever-widening horizons. It is also like climbing a mountain peak where we have to watch every step in moving up, while simultaneously being taken in by breath-taking views. Such 'guides' have been known as *lam-rim* (Stages on the Path) in Tibet, and an extensive literature on this subject has been preserved.

The earliest work of this kind is attributed to Guru Padmasambhava, a person whose historicity has been overshadowed by myths and legends, all of which attest to the impact his presentation of Buddhist ideas has had on those who came under their spell. What distinguishes his work (as well as those works that developed in the tradition initiated by him and known as the Nyingma order) from the works of the same nature in other schools of thought, is the vividness of presentation. It is the presentation of lived-through experience, not a stale piling up of quotations from canonical texts. The same vividness and directness the reader will find in this book whose author is one of the foremost Nyingma scholars.

Openness Mind has been written for those who dare to ask questions which touch on the meaning of life, and it has taken form from out of such questions asked.

Needless to point out that the title itself is a challenge —to open up ourselves is to have mind restored to its creative openness. *Openness Mind* certainly points the way in that direction.

Herbert V. Guenther
University of Saskatchewan

Preface

In this new volume of essays, I have drawn material from seven years of beginning and advanced meditation classes and seminars given at the Nyingma Institute. Among those attending these courses were professionals studying new approaches to healing and to psychological growth, as well as those who simply wished to extend their spiritual understanding.

Meditation is the common ground of many and varied interests. It is a vast and complex subject, aimed at the development of an understanding of the mind, an understanding which we can carry into the whole of our experience. Meditation is not a withdrawal from life, it is an extension: we can take it with us to enrich whatever we do, wherever we go.

This concept is basic to the Nyingma teachings, which are designed to provide inner strength and self-reliance. Readers of *Gesture of Balance* may recognize certain of these themes in this new volume, but while my first volume of essays was designed mainly as an introduction to the various aspects of meditation, *Openness Mind*, as the title suggests, moves more deeply into the nature of the mind.

It is most important to learn how to use our minds to make our lives balanced and healthy. These days there is a great deal of emphasis on the influence of the environment on our health and state of mind, but there is little comprehension of the influence our states of mind have on the environment. When we have understanding of the nature of the mind, we can approach the problem of life with a sureness and integrity that give a wholesome quality to all we do. We interrelate smoothly and flowingly with the world around us.

By means of meditation we can teach our minds to be calm and balanced; within this calmness is a richness and a potential, an inner knowledge which can render our lives boundlessly satisfying and meaningful. We can tap the healing qualities of our minds. While the mind may be what traps us in unhealthy patterns of stress and imbalance, it is also the mind which can free us.

Within the mind we can find the sense of purpose and the abilities which can bring meaning to our lives. We can learn to deal readily and effectively with what have seemed to be insolvable problems, by bringing to them the simple techniques we learn in meditation. The mind can become a familiar and useful tool which we can put

to use for the enrichment of our experience. In this way, as we bring balance to our inner environment, our outer environment becomes balanced as well. We learn self-reliance, the natural freedom of mind.

The Nyingma tradition of Tibetan Buddhism emphasizes this approach to meditation which opens to the world. The teachings of the Nyingma tradition are a unique blend of the Hinayana and its emphasis on individualistic concern, effort, and responsibility, the Mahayana and its emphasis on the development of compassion and openness, and the Vajrayana method of transcending both positive and negative, so that all we do becomes the material out of which we create a beneficial and balanced life. The Vajrayana seems especially suited to the people of the West who are constantly enmeshed in the everyday cares and concerns of the world.

It is my hope that this book will help others along the path of growth and self-discovery so that they may better cope with these troubled times. This is far from a complete presentation of the Nyingma teachings, but I have tried to convey the many facets of these teachings and their open view. Mind is as vast as all space, and the approach to its understanding should be as wide.

Gesture of Balance brought such a positive response from its readers that I was encouraged to offer a slightly more advanced presentation of meditation in this new volume of essays. Those who adopted *Gesture of Balance* for their classes in Buddhism and Philosophy should therefore find even more helpful material in *Openness Mind*.

I have spent the last year concentrating on writing instead of teaching. I feel that this will be, in the long run, more helpful to my friends and students—a class is over in a few weeks, while we can keep a book for many years.

In *Openness Mind*, each essay has been chosen with this intent: to open ways for the reader to enrich himself. In order to present as much material as possible, and to make the text as clear as possible, many of my students and friends have read the manuscript, using their many different backgrounds and interests to make suggestions for clarifying, and adding to, both the language and meaning. I would like to thank all those who participated in this process. I am also very grateful to all those of Dharma Publishing and Dharma Press who put so much care into the production of this book.

I hope that *Openness Mind* will be of value to many. I dedicate any benefit deriving from this work to the peace of all mankind.

PART ONE

Openness

Learning through Experience

Meditation is a way of opening our lives to the richness of experience, not an esoteric practice limited to certain times and places. Whether we live in the quiet of the country or in the turmoil of the city, meditation can actually become a way of life. In this kind of meditation, we learn to embrace and learn from whatever we experience.

This all-embracing form of meditation, however, is not as easy as it sounds, for it entails mindfulness in all we do. From the simple act of getting up in the morning to our dreams at night, everything is included in this meditation. We learn to open our senses to each nuance of experience, mindful of even the smallest details of our lives, such as how we walk and how we talk with others. In this way, we learn to open to the truth of our experience. How we live, what is happening in our lives, how we are affected by our experience—this is the ground of reality, and the source of spiritual awareness.

We can cultivate this awareness in every aspect of our lives—in our work, our relationships, and even in our abilities. All of these are potential teachers that we can open to and learn from when we see the possibilities for growth inherent in all we do.

As we learn from our experience, our appreciation of life increases; our senses grow keener, our minds grow more clear and more perceptive. Developing awareness, concentration, honesty, caring, and openness can become an enlightening experience that will not only benefit ourselves, but will build qualities that can serve as guidelines to those around us.

As our awareness develops, our entire frame of reference slowly becomes transformed. We see the interrelationships of thought and action, and consequently become more sensitive in our communication with others. Our observations penetrate to deeper levels—we discover how feelings are produced, and how thought functions. As our awareness deepens even further, we can even perceive the link between past, present, and future, and therefore learn to pattern our actions so that our lives are satisfied and fulfilled.

At first, however, our vision is limited: it is not easy to determine what the results of our actions will be. We can follow the guidelines of society, but few of these have been created with more than a shortsighted aim and result in view. So although the results of our actions may seem to be good at the time, in the long run they may turn out to be harmful. In frustration we may try to force our will on situations, making the outlook even worse.

Mindfulness, by contrast, opens our vision to more constructive action. And patience allows room for our new vision to work. Patience works silently, like a secret agent, to protect us from getting caught up in pointless action and despair. When we consciously develop patience, it can become a natural and appropriate response to each new situation; we strengthen ourselves for even the most difficult times.

When patience is strongly developed, awareness appears even from within our negativities, and from that awareness comes our meditation. We see that everything that occurs is a manifestation of energy, which itself is a form of our awareness, and we realize that all experience, each of the twenty-four hours of the day, is a part of the enlightenment nature.

This awareness is accessible to all who search for it; it can always be reached by delving into the nature of experience. Our experience can take us far beyond our ordinary thinking, seeing, and being. It can take us to enlightenment itself.

When we reach a state where we are truly aware, we are like a lotus flower: the lotus is pure and beautiful, though it grows from the mud. Once we are aware, we can function properly even amid the confusions of the world. Our positive attitude benefits both ourselves and others; we *live* the truth that we have acquired.

Samsara is like a poisonous fruit. We eat and enjoy it, but in the end it will kill us, unless we can transmute the poison. Nothing on the samsaric level can ultimately give us freedom and contentment or truly fulfill our desires. But when we live according to an enlightened view, the poison will not harm us because nirvana is 'within' samsara. They are the same. But this may be very difficult to understand without first knowing how to transmute the emotions and how to transcend our obstacles. When we can do this, then all that we do will be helpful. But until then, although many of our activities may seem satisfying, we are just accumulating more karma—more needs and more hindering patterns.

Student: But you have said that we should not avoid any experience.

Rinpoche: This is true once we are more aware, once we are strong enough to recognize the consequences of our actions. First, however, we need to learn how samsara works, how we accumulate pain and frustration. We begin to see that there is no peace, no pleasure, nothing desirable in the way we have been living, and that our experience is somehow always spoiled by worry, guilt, or anxiety. Once we realize this, we see there is no other alternative than to become enlightened, to become free from samsara. We cannot return to our ignorance.

Student: Still, I think we have a role to play in life and that most of us cannot escape being in the world. We cannot just walk away from everything. In the West, legal situations make this almost impossible.

Rinpoche: Therefore we have to accept responsibility for our commitments and our karma. Whether we are free or not depends upon our view and how we work in the world. We can learn to transform negative situations. Samsara, we might say, is our training ground. However, Buddha taught that samsara offers no peace. We have to suffer, grow old, and eventually die. Everyone has to go through this, but very few are ready to accept this truth. Impermanence is one of the root causes of suffering, and mental anxiety can seem even more painful than physical sickness. Even the most beautiful monastery or temple, or the most beautiful human body, still belongs to samsara, and samsara will destroy it.

Student: But even though nothing lasts, it seems important to enjoy the flower or to taste whatever is impermanent for as long as it lasts.

Rinpoche: Yes, our body is like a rented house, and unless we use it, it has no value to us. But it seems important to know how to use our lives constructively. Life is temporary and very valuable. We do not have much time to waste. We can use our lives well . . . or waste our time looking for pleasures and satisfactions that just increase our craving and frustration when we do not have them. Like bees, we can go from flower to flower, but what will we do when all the flowers have faded? By learning how to be totally satisfied every moment, our time will never be wasted.

Student: Still, I don't see how to bridge the gap between ignoring or rejecting the world, and making our spiritual path part of the world and helping other people—the ideal of the Bodhisattva.

Rinpoche: We must be able to put our theories into practice; we must be able to go beyond ego. Yet the ego is very hard to give up. We may be able to do it for a couple of minutes, but how can we function for a whole lifetime, or even just a whole day, without ego!

The Buddha had great understanding of the mind at all of its various levels and stages of development. His teachings are therefore not limited to only one way; they have many different aspects. One and the same teaching can be a beginning practice to one person, and yet a more advanced instruction to another. There are also many 'inner' teachings that are understood according to the experience and understanding of each individual.

Student: When I choose to look at the world from the viewpoint of my ego and identity, I can see that I have created the situations around me.

Rinpoche: Good. But then what is your situation and what do you do about it?

Student: My ideal, and sometimes my action, is that I will perform right action out of love and understanding.

Rinpoche: But to perform right action you must be aware from moment to moment. How do you start?

Student: All the time.

Rinpoche: Yes, but that's a big job. Only a very awakened person can perform right action with every single thought. Not very many people can do it. We may be growing in wisdom and knowledge each day, but the process still takes a great deal of time and is very hard work. It must be more important to us than anything else.

Your attitude is very positive, and I don't want to discourage you, but even the Mahayana says that it takes thirty-three kalpas—many, many lifetimes—to reach enlightenment. We can see the importance of always acting wisely, and even try to do this, but our attachments still get in the way. Sometimes our mouths are faster than our hearts.

According to the Mahayana, however, once the initial wish to become enlightened arises in the mind, something happens unconsciously within us. At first, we may actually work against this wish and create more suffering for ourselves, but it is through this suffering that we can eliminate many obstacles and wake up.

Once we begin to seek enlightenment, there is no turning back; the positive influence of this wish for enlightenment is very great. But we need to learn how to proceed most effectively. Our intentions may be good, but carrying out our intentions may be difficult. What do you do with your samsaric attachments to food, entertainment, or lovers?

Student: I have begun to be detached from them.

Rinpoche: Do you reject these things? How are you detached?

Student: It's an attitude . . .

Rinpoche: Your dissatisfaction may be leading you to renounce what you don't really enjoy. Dissatisfaction is very different from detachment. We can easily give up what we find dissatisfying, but it is difficult to renounce other things. Eating, sleeping, and enjoying ourselves are very important to us. If you take away enjoyment, then what do you have?

The world is always with us. But we don't know what it will present us with tomorrow: it is always changing. We may be happy, or joyful, or suffering and in pain. In other words, we can't trust our feelings to stay the same from one day to the next. Tomorrow may be a very peaceful day, and you may be very happy just as you are.

Student: Sometimes when I sit down to meditate, meditation doesn't seem so important. The world seems more important. Why is that?

Rinpoche: Maybe you are beginning to touch yourself. The world *is* important—you have to help. Encourage yourself not to retire into your meditation, but to reach out to others. When we make compassion our practice, we become full of joy.

Student: Then no matter what I do, it's still samsaric.

Rinpoche: Maybe that is all there is.

Student: What I am finding out is that the way I have been living and the things that I have done, at best, still leave me empty.

Rinpoche: Yes. Ultimately, everything is empty. That is the basic teaching. But this is not necessarily a negative point of view. Buddhism is not a negative philosophy. In talking about suffering, Buddhism is just trying to deal with the way things are. The teachings advise us to understand our suffering thoroughly, so that we will not need it any more.

Often we prevent ourselves from seeing our situation clearly; we do not want to take responsibility for our actions. Or else we are afraid to change, because it is too threatening to our security. Suffering may be the only way we can wake up and clearly see the nature of our samsaric condition. The more ready we are to admit to the reality of suffering in our lives, the more necessary it becomes to do something about it.

Student: We are Westerners, without a traditional model for these understandings. How can we gain the openness we need just to live in society?

Rinpoche: I think Westerners can automatically understand many of Buddha's beginning teachings because there is a lot of frustration here. We can understand a great deal just by studying our own life experiences. The Buddha himself acquired wisdom through the natural course of living. But this way takes a long time, so we may wish to benefit from the Buddha's teachings. Often, however, Westerners have the concept that Buddhism is a 'religion', that you have to believe blindly, without understanding; that you have to follow someone else's rules. But Buddhism or the Dharma is actually the understanding of reality; it is verifiable through our own experience.

Student: I seem to be studying myself, not a religion.
Rinpoche: That's why the Buddhadharma can be applicable to everyone. All living beings have the opportunity to experience for themselves the truth of what the Buddha discovered.

The Self-Image

Our natural state of being is awareness: an awareness which is not *of* anything, but which is an all-encompassing state of pure experience. Within awareness our minds are balanced, light, free, and flexible. We are not, however, able to stay in this awareness, for our immediate inclination is to want to know *who* is experiencing *what*. As a result, awareness gives way to our ordinary consciousness which divides our perceptions into subject and object, creating as subject a 'self-image', the 'I'. But what actually is this 'I'? Can we actually find it anywhere in the mind? When we look carefully, we see that the 'I' is simply an image which the mind has projected. This 'I' has no reality in itself, yet we take it as real, and let it run our lives. The 'I' then obscures our awareness and separates us from our experience by dividing it into a subjective and an objective pole.

Under the influence of the self-image we perpetuate this subject-object orientation. As soon as we identify, comparison begins; grasping and selfishness rapidly follow. Then the mind makes discriminations and judgments, which cause conflicts. The self-image gives energy to these conflicts, and these conflicts in turn feed the self-image. The self-image thus perpetuates itself, tending to filter experience in ways that allow only its own rigid constructions room to function. Neither open nor accepting, the self-image imprisons us in blockages and constrictions. Our natural flow of energy is interrupted, and the range of our responsiveness and the depth of our experience are severely limited.

To free ourselves from the interference of the self-image so that our natural balance can have room to function, we must first see that the self-image is not a genuine part of us, that we do not need it, and that, in fact, the self-image obscures our true being. One way to do this is to step back and observe our thoughts whenever we are in the midst of emotional ferment.

Even when we are very upset, it is possible to separate ourselves from the pain of the emotion. Stand back and actually look at the pain. With this knowledge, you can see that the disturbance is actually the operation of the self-image. You may even see that much of your unhappiness was the result of the self-image leading you to have expectations which could not be fulfilled. The self-image is a kind of fantasy itself, so it tends to build a fantasy world. This fantasizing arouses a great deal of energy, and when these fantasies do not come true, the energy is blocked, and turns into frustration.

We can find all sorts of rational reasons for our difficulties, but an honest look can go beyond these reasons to discover that our unhappiness comes from identifying with the self-image and following its dictates. The self-image dominates and controls us, so that we are caught in its power and lose our independence.

Even when we see our predicament, and try consciously to stop our suffering, our self-image often leads us to repeat painful experiences again and again. We may not really want to change. The attachment to a self-image is powerful: we may not want to seek new alternatives because we sense a possible loss of our 'identity'.

We often actually cling to our suffering, for suffering seems to offer more security than opening to real change. Yet to experience genuine happiness and balance in our lives, we have to give up the root cause of our suffering: the self-image.

The instant we stop serving the self-image and its needs, all our difficulties disappear, and our energy is released to flow smoothly. This energy can then be used to further enhance our understanding of ourselves.

Go back into your emotions, and intentionally make them as vivid as you can, letting the sensations grow more and more intense. Look at the grasping nature of the self-image: it is always making demands, always wanting more and more. By feeding the self-image, we perpetuate what we can never essentially satisfy. In the end, we have difficulty finding any satisfaction, for the grasping turns satisfaction into frustration.

Frustration leads to negative feelings, but any negativity is in conflict with the inherent positive quality of mental energy. The transformation of negative feelings occurs naturally when we cultivate a positive and accepting attitude toward all experience. The resulting energy can make us more creative, more aware, more open to learning. This energy can counter the action of the self-image which feeds on negativity and redoubles its strength with each frustration it undergoes.

As soon as we know the self-image for what it is, we know that we can change, that we can develop flexibility in our attitudes without giving up anything. This change is possible because our consciousness is by its nature not fixed, but flexible.

We can develop this flexibility by adopting new perspectives. For example, every time you feel unhappy, say "I am happy." Say it strongly to yourself, even if your feelings contradict you. Remember, it is your self-image that is unhappy, not you. It is possible to switch instantly to a happy, balanced attitude, and to stay there by believing it. There is this choice when you are open to a positive attitude. Your whole inner quality can change, even if the external conditions do not.

Another way to counter the self-image is to become immersed in the unhappiness, feel it and believe it, and then switch it swiftly, electrically, like a fish darting in water, to happiness. First, be the experience, completely accept it. Then, jump to the opposite extreme. How is it? It is possible to clearly see the differences between the positive and negative experience, and sometimes to experience both at the same time. By jumping mentally from positive to negative and then back again, it is possible to see that both are manifestations of awareness, and as such have a 'neutral' energy which can be used in any way.

In the beginning, try to gain skill in this switching technique. You can see what you are feeling now and how it was before, sometimes feeling the two different situations simultaneously. This technique thus teaches acceptance, making it possible to have positive feelings about any experience that occurs.

It is our choice: to follow the self-image which makes us its prisoners, or to develop a positive attitude which brings lightness, fullness, and wholeness. On the positive side, no expectations, no frustrations, no dominating self-image takes us away from the immediacy of our being. Obstacles and distractions no longer divide our feelings and our mind. We are balanced and experience ourselves complete just as we are.

No matter what situation we find ourselves in, we can choose our mental environment. And choosing balance will give life purpose. The choice is ours; we have only to choose the way of freedom.

Self-Change

The pattern of life is frustration: it casts a shadow on our leisure and our work. Although our lives may seem to be happy on the surface, a sense of deep dissatisfaction or incompleteness may linger underneath, a sense for which we can find no definite cause. When we think about it, however, we see that this sense comes from knowing that we are not using our lives as productively as we could. It is so easy to put off doing what we know is important or even meaningful for our lives. But waiting for the future is like waiting for a bus that never comes. Unless we soon start doing what we feel is important, we will get nowhere. Taking action, however, is not an easy task, because it means taking charge of our lives and learning to be honest with ourselves in unaccustomed ways.

We have unknowingly developed patterns of action which have come to assume a force of their own. Later, we notice with surprise that this force, karma, has in a real sense taken over the running of our lives in an almost automatic manner, and that we have allowed ourselves to lose control over the direction of our lives. Our opportunities slip away, and the slipping away also forms a pattern; the rest of our life may simply consist of living out patterns that serve no real purpose.

This loss of control comes about in subtle but definite ways. For example, not doing what we know we should do strengthens a pattern of avoidance. This reluctance becomes a habit. We begin to automatically avoid anything even slightly difficult or unpleasant—challenging and productive opportunities may be lost, for the pattern of avoidance has made our decisions for us. As the pattern strengthens, we weaken ourselves still further.

As time passes, these patterns grow stronger and stronger and even continue throughout other lifetimes, whether or not we remember them. This is karma, and it is a part of the process of life. Because of this karma, it becomes increasingly difficult to achieve our goals, to find fulfillment, or to progress spiritually. Our lives are not truly healthful, yet we have so internalized these patterns, unhealthy as they are, that it is not easy to change. This patterning, escaping any notice, has become a part of us.

How can we undo these patterns? First, we need to simply recognize them. Then, by identifying our habits, we can take away their covert power to determine our lives. This can end our excuses and initiate an honest and active responsibility for our lives—replacing our tendency to passively yearn for a perfect place, a Shangri-la where life is free from problems.

We cannot change overnight, but we can start a process which will build up momentum, a process which will give us a solid, genuine quality that will help us to become more vital, more balanced. We begin by breaking the patterns of avoidance. We can concentrate regularly on work that we do not want to do, and then meditate informally on the emotions which arise from doing this work, emotions such as anger or frustration.

Stay with any such emotion; taste it with meditation. Practice until a feeling comes from behind the original emotion, a feeling manifesting itself at first as physical tightness or strain. As you keep penetrating your resistance, the feeling may intensify. Finally, you will recognize the feeling as fear.

Fear is elusive. Most of us do not readily accept that fear guides our choices and our actions. The sense of being in control of our lives is part of our cherished self-image, a self-image we want to protect. We feel secure in our established patterns; we fear the uncertain and the unknown as threatening to these patterns. By yielding to this fear, even when unaware of it, we reinforce it. Fear thus creates more fear, and becomes a subtle propelling force. What may seem to us a situation over which we have no control can actually be our fear of

confronting what is within ourselves. This fear can per-
vade our lives.

When we contact our fear and recognize it, we can see
that most of our rationalizations, our petty likes and dis-
likes, even the personality quirks we so enjoy, are all simply
ego-supporting devices serving to hide our having given
in to fear. These apparently harmless inclinations reveal
their real power as karmic patterns at work—patterns
which have concealed our true motivations so cleverly
that we have lost the capacity to be truly honest with
ourselves. When we have this insight, we must act on it,
for it is at this point that we have the knowledge and the
opportunity to break through our limitations.

To break these patterns we must experience our fear
directly. We can challenge the concept of fear itself,
penetrating it by means of meditation. We enter into our
fear. As our consciousness goes into the emotion, we stop
labeling the sensation as fear, and we become aware that
what we are feeling is simply energy. The surrounding
tension then breaks, enabling us to relax and to set this
energy free. This release leaves us calm and at peace with
ourselves.

By going through fear in meditation, we can learn to
be effective in situations where before we could not even
act. We can break through our "not wanting to do." We
need only contact the feeling of such situations directly:
patiently, quietly, confidently. This pattern is genuinely
healthy, truly enabling us to determine our actions and
our lives.

In understanding the patterns of karma, we make life a great opportunity. Human existence is precious; when we free ourselves from our automatic responses, we can realize its boundless potential. It is only a matter of finding the silent places that lie beyond the patterns, of contacting our true natures, and then of nourishing their growth. We do this by learning to be honest with ourselves. Although this breaking of old patterns does not happen in one day, it will come when, moment by moment, we learn to maintain balance in our lives.

Transforming Fear

From childhood with its fear of the dark to old age with its fear of death, fear is a normal part of our lives. But suppose we question our fears. When we study fear calmly, we make a remarkable discovery: fear is a creation of our minds. We label a certain feeling 'fear', give it a specific character and definition, and establish rules about how we will react to it. We create a pattern of fearing which takes on a reality all its own.

Simply understanding 'reasons' for our fears in an attempt to control them only strikes at the symptoms, not the cause. The real source of fear lies in our minds —adding more thoughts and concepts only supports the pattern of fear. We need a different approach.

Fear is nothing but misapplied energy, a mental projection, an idea. When our body reacts to fear, the body itself is not afraid. The fear comes from concepts and thoughts that we have learned to associate with this reaction. Although a concept cannot exist as a solid entity, the concept can be so convincing that we believe in it; when we believe in it, we give the concept power over us whether it is real or not.

The shadow of fear is always hiding in the gap between our subjective and objective worlds. We have the fear of losing ourselves, of losing our identity. We have such attachment to our concepts of who and what we are that we are afraid of their possible disruption.

We can loosen some of fear's hold on us through meditation. Meditation relaxes our usual subject-object orientation; in meditation, internal dialogue is quieted, and when thoughts arise, we do not follow them or attach interpretations to them. Thus when fear or any other thought arises, we simply let it come and go, remaining relaxed and calm. We can let the fear pass through us, and the meditative state stays undisturbed.

Yet meditation also can open up various blockages, so at times it releases powerful energy. Unaccustomed to such a powerful surge, we may think it poses some threat. We then label this manifestation fear, and give it a form. Now we have to break through the thought of 'fear' to unfreeze that energy.

It helps to remember that fear is only an association; fear does not exist until a feeling is labeled and objectified as such. When we can let go of our concepts and expectations, there is nothing to be afraid of. As we observe our fears, we can see that they form no essential part of our natures, but instead are patterns that we have constructed. Simply recognizing the pattern of fear helps us to understand how we are being trapped by an illusion. With this understanding we can relax and begin to open to the energy within our hearts; we can face our fears directly. This signals that we have made our experience our meditation. We open naturally to further experience, confident in our meditation and its resilience.

Seeing that our fears do nothing but restrict our energy can give us tremendous power and strength, enabling us to discover the true dynamism of our consciousness. Nothing in the physical world can protect us from objects of fear; transcending fear itself through meditation is our true protection.

Long ago, in Tibet, those who wished to conquer fear would actually go to cemeteries and sleep among the corpses. They would deliberately allow their imaginations to run wild so as to become terrified, and then they would confront their fear and try to integrate it within their minds. By penetrating fear, they were able to tap the great power centered within their being, and use it for meditation. In this way, they developed freedom from fear.

The insubstantiality of fear may be understood philosophically, but that does us little good. We must experientially understand what fear is. Then life becomes playful.

There is a true story about a lama who was learning to be a practicing *chod*, a person who learns to conquer all fear. *Chod* training involves three or four months of practice, at the end of which a student goes alone to a cemetery every night for one week, and there performs a certain practice. The student carries a drum, called a *damaru*, a bell, and a horn made out of human bones which is used for calling demons. When the horn is blown, the student calls out to the demons, "Come, eat my body!" The villagers are always frightened when they hear the horns blown.

The cemetery to which this lama was sent was in a grassy valley, surrounded by high mountains. It was a windy, lonely place, empty except for outcroppings of barren rock and the screams of wild dogs.

Now this particular lama had been bragging about his powers. For three days he had gone on and on, telling how the demons had come to him, and how he had subdued them. He was a very proud man, but many respected him because he was a healer. The last night of his week at the cemetery, a group of young lamas who did not like him decided to watch and see exactly how he performed his practice.

Tibetan cemeteries are scary places. The bodies are put on rocks, tied to stakes, and left for the vultures. The vultures leave the hair and the bones. There is a strong, foul stench.

The young lamas, hiding behind clusters of large rocks, saw the *chod* practitioner go to the center of the cemetery where he placed a pillow on a rock and sat down. After it had grown dark, the lama began to blow his horn and call out, "All demons, come! All gods, come! Eat my arms and legs! I am ready to give all my body to you!" Loudly he called again and again, "Demons, come to me now, eat my body!" He was praying very seriously and reciting mantras.

The young lamas put a sulphur paste on their faces and hands, so that they glowed. Then, whistling softly as they came, they crawled slowly toward him. At first he did not notice: he was so busy blowing his horn and praying loudly. Then he saw the glowing faces in the grass, moving toward him from every direction. More and more loudly he rang his bell and beat his drum. Again he looked nervously around, and prayed faster and faster. But the glowing faces moved closer and closer.

Finally, he threw everything into the air, and holding the skirts of his robe, he ran off, dropping his *damaru*. The *damaru* broke and his bell broke, and he fled terrified from the cemetery.

The next day the lama's teachers asked as usual about his experience of the night before. They also asked where his beautiful *damaru* was that he prayed with in the morning. Every morning before he had told how he had conversed with demons and how cleverly he had subdued them. But this time he said nothing. He later gave up the *chod* practice entirely.

When we practice, it sometimes seems that there are real demons and real fears. We can control them as simple mental events, but when frightening situations arise, it is harder to cope with fear. We may not be attacked by demons in physical form, but there are all kinds of different obstacles that can arise. Even though they have no substance, when we accept them as being real, we make them so.

As soon as we see problems arising, we can act; when we are always alert for obstacles, we can challenge them early and protect ourselves. Consider death. We do not like to even think about death, yet the time will come when we will be separated from our bodies, when we will find ourselves alone in our consciousness. At the end, our lives will seem like one night's dream—a very long dream, with all kinds of experiences, but still a one-night's dream.

That we have to die is not a pleasant thought, but if we overcome our reluctance to think about it, and develop awareness of death, we can protect ourselves from the fear and mental confusion that occur when death catches us by surprise. Suddenly we are forced to give up our family, friends, loved ones, and possessions. When death comes, nothing can help us: at that time, our intelligence, our beauty, our money, and our power are of no avail. We realize again how beautiful our world is—the gardens, the trees, the mountains, the people—and with this realization follows the profound regret that we only really appreciate living when we are at the point of dying. Life is incredibly beautiful. But we have to leave this beautiful place; we cannot even take our bodies with us.

The fear of death is extremely powerful; it is far more intense than any other emotion. When faced with death, we may try to ignore it or to pray, but nothing really helps. More potent even than the physical pain is the pain of fear. Even the word 'death' seems frightening to us, because it connotes an end. We may believe that the consciousness and the body are the same, and that if the body dies then consciousness must also cease. Even if we believe that our consciousness survives after our body dies, we know that in death they must separate, and the thought of giving up our body makes us feel very lost and afraid.

But as our understanding of the meaning of human existence increases, it is possible to see that death is not a separation but a transformation. When we can widen our perspective, we can see that life cannot be lost and it cannot disappear. With the development of understanding, fear fades. Death becomes a very good teacher.

Life and death are parts of an indefinitely continuing process of subtle change and re-creation; this process is like a wheel which always turns. Once we have established our karmic patterns, we do not consciously have to add momentum to the wheel—it turns on its own. When we begin to understand this process, then death no longer seems so frightening, because we know that we will have another chance as the wheel continues to turn. As with any fear, it is the label that generates the fear, not the object of the fear itself.

When we let go of labeling our experiences as being joy or pain, youth or age, life or death—we can find a certain detached interest in them. We can even be playful with them. We can assume different perspectives at will; no fear of any particular experience dominates us. At this level, death becomes just another word for another experience.

Unfortunately, in America death is a taboo subject. It would be helpful to us if death were more openly acknowledged as a natural part of being, not as a great tragedy. By understanding the impermanence of life, we can fully value each moment. Awareness of death teaches us to enjoy life, not possessively or emotionally, but simply, by being filled with the beauty and creativity of living fully.

As we realize our responsibility to make the most of our lives, we can deal more easily with the idea of death. When we view death as a transformation rather than as an ending, the pervasive fear of death loses its hold on us, and the energy once caught up in the fear is no longer blocked. We can then use this energy to be more keenly aware of the beauty inherent in the rich texture of our experience. We will have no regrets when we come to die.

We will know ourselves as part of the nature of being, part of the cosmos, in this present life and after.

Our human bodies are precious vehicles for growth and experience, the only medium through which we can become enlightened. But we must use our human bodies for this purpose, for at the time of death our best friend is an enlightened mind.

Our task, then, is to strengthen our meditation, to make a crystal of our minds, so that there is no separation between inner and outer. Then, with some insight into the nature of enlightenment, all fears dissolve, even the most powerful of fears, the fear of death. Channels toward enlightenment open, and our whole being changes. Before, we were sleeping a fearful, fitful sleep; now we are waking up. As soon as we awaken fully, we will realize the enlightened quality of our natural mind.

Meditation: Let It Be

Buddha's teaching is a way of life. It is a path for living a balanced, peaceful, and useful life: a path which provides us with a way out of the endless series of problems and struggles we face in life. We can discover this path in meditation, a way which opens us to the meaning of enlightenment.

Although meditation is actually very simple, it is easy to get confused by the many different descriptions of meditative practices. Forget them all and just sit quietly. Be very still and relaxed, and do not try to do anything. Let everything—thoughts, feelings, and concepts—go through your mind unheeded. Do not grasp at ideas or thoughts as they come and go or try to manipulate them. When you feel you have to do something in your meditation, you only make it harder. Let meditation do itself.

After we learn to let thoughts slip by, the thoughts will slow down, and nearly disappear. Then, behind the flow of thoughts, you will sense a feeling which is the foundation of meditation. When you contact this quiet place behind your inner dialogues, let your awareness of it grow stronger. You can then simply rest in the silence. For in that silence there is nothing to do; there is no reason to produce anything or to stop anything. Just let everything be.

When meditating in this simple, accepting way, the meditative quality gradually becomes more pronounced, and its experience more immediate. After each meditation the light of this experience will remain and strengthen with practice. Meditation just comes of itself, like the morning sun; inner awareness, once touched upon, radiates naturally. But finding this inner awareness needs daily practice, so it is important to set aside time for meditation.

As you persevere in your practice, you will know whether you are on the right path, and whether your meditation is effective, by examining your life. When your mind is peaceful and more loving, when your emotions are steady and even, and your life is going smoothly, then you know that you are making progress.

The inner quiet which arises from meditation relieves the stress of these times of rapid change, when it is so easy to lose our sense of stability and balance. In trying to do too much in too little time, we can become agitated and upset. But when our minds are relaxed and quiet, life becomes simple and balanced, free from disruptive extremes. When we are balanced, we are healthy—the body is relaxed and the mind peaceful. We become free from confusions, disappointments, and illusions. We learn to guide ourselves with our meditation experience.

Balance is central even in our relationship to the spiritual teachings. The Dharma, for instance, is a little like many colleges and universities—all kinds of interesting subjects are offered, and we can waste our time and energy trying to learn them all. One of the great masters once said that knowledge is like the stars at night—we cannot count such vastness. So it is better not to try to do everything at once, even spiritually.

At first, it is important to concentrate on those teachings that are most immediately relevant to us—teachings for which we have the background. Otherwise we waste our time, and gain only frustration. Be content with proceeding gradually, step by step, keeping motivation strong and persevering in meditation practice. It is very true that in developing meditation, the slowest way is the fastest way. When we cultivate our meditation carefully, without forcing, the results will always be clear: although we may not sense each day's growth, the growth is steady. This path is not like pouring rain, which forces us to shelter, but more like snow gently blanketing the land.

Make your meditation casual, open—not self-conscious or forced. Then meditation experiences will come. Experiences in themselves are not so valuable, but they can be a form of extension to the meditation; certain experiences can touch the subtleties of the mind, and help to clarify the nature of existence.

Student: I have a very strong will and I often use it to will myself to relax or to endure painful situations. What is the right place or direction or use of will in meditation?
Rinpoche: That is the whole problem. There is no need of will in meditation. The common idea of willing is to make an effort. Most people find it hard not to make an effort, not to do something in meditation. But will does not help; the mind is sensitive and cannot be forced. As soon as we try to force the mind, our meditation is disturbed.

Student: Then how do we try?
Rinpoche: Bring a lighter quality to your meditation. Then when pain or the ego-image or anything else disturbs you, it will be much easier to transcend. When your meditation has a heavy, 'willed' quality, you may not be able to progress. Heaviness is wanting something a certain way. We want a specific condition, feeling, possession, identity—a little nest. We want to be in a certain place, and that wanting has a heaviness. It is limited, narrow, specific; it is bound by identities, so consequently the ego is also involved.

Lightness is transparent, like a crystal. It has no particular place, it does not belong anywhere. Lightness is free, like the sun. In meditation, there is no awareness of subject and object. There can be no will, for there is no longer anyone to hold on to anything. There is no subjective orientation. The subject is transcended; all that is left is meditation, only experience. Try to develop that kind of attitude.

Student: At that point is formal meditation necessary? When there is no subject and object, everything must be meditation.

Rinpoche: When your life is free of problems, and you are always in the meditative state, then formal meditation is not so important. You are then free of conflicting thoughts, free of emotion, free of identity. Yet at the same time, you can act effectively. That is meditative knowledge, which is different from ordinary knowledge.

To gain ordinary knowledge, we always need to make an effort. When we try, we learn, and then we experience. But in meditation, although we must make some effort in the beginning, once meditation is entered, there is no need for further effort. That is why we use the word 'be' . . . because 'be' means we *are* the meditation. Once in meditation, time itself is transcended. There is no past, there is no future, not even a present.

Student: Is it really possible to reach a place where there is no time?

Rinpoche: Yes. As soon as you can stay in the space between thoughts, there is no time.

Student: And when you come out and you move around in the world, there is still no time?

Rinpoche: When you move, it may be different. Moving

brings you back into the relative world, back to thoughts, where time again exists.

Student: But it lowers your anxiety when you know you can always be in no time, doesn't it? Even if you move around, you don't have the same urgency or pain or emotions, do you?
Rinpoche: Sometimes you may have what is called a mystic experience. Then a special light may appear. Then there is no time; all ordinary concepts are transcended.

Student: I can see that happening for brief times in meditation. But I'm talking about in the living of life.
Rinpoche: Meditation is living life time. It is happening within this life. But you can expand that understanding; you can widen your experience, and make less effort. Then it is possible to have that meditation experience anytime.

Student: Since I've begun meditating, I find that I'm less attached. I don't care whether things get done or not, yet they need to be done. What should I do?
Rinpoche: I think that you are enjoying your meditation so much that you don't care about anything else. But when we live in this world, we have to maintain our lives. Learn to develop your awareness during your working time—be calm and mindful, don't let yourself be rushed or pressured. You will enjoy your work more and accept it as part of meditation. This attitude will make it a little easier.

Student: Time seems to go more slowly during meditation.

Rinpoche: This indicates that your meditation is developing. You are entering the experiential level. Our minds usually jump here and there, so when you find time slowing down, your meditation is improving.

Time does not move in just two directions. Linear time is the relationship between two points, but at the experiential level of inner consciousness, time becomes many-dimensional: forward, backward, up, and down. Time as we ordinarily think of it involves the relative aspects of past, present, and future. We believe that as long as we are experiencing the present, the future cannot yet be, and that as soon as the present shifts, the future comes to take its place. But within meditation, we actually become the experience and these relative aspects of time no longer exist.

We usually look at memory in the same way that we look at ordinary time—we believe that memory is linear. We think we can experience memories only one after another. But once our experience widens, we realize that we have only been seeing in one dimension. From a more sensitive, fuller perspective, the dimensions of experience multiply.

Student: When I used to meditate several hours a day, I would have flashes of insight which would push me forward. But I don't have those any more. I wonder if having those insights again would spur me on?

Rinpoche: In beginning meditation we believe that experiences belong to the mind or consciousness, and this leads to a kind of experiential longing. As long as we remain on this level of the relative mind reporting back to itself or trying to convince the ego of progress, then we may need such experiences. But once we are able to let go of our meditation experience so that there is no longer a sense of ownership or identity, then having experiences or not no longer matters.

PART TWO

Deepening through Meditation

The Deepening Stream

We occasionally experience great joy, but only rarely. Because we usually feel unfulfilled, we tend to fall into the habit of daydreaming about the future, or drifting back into the past. It is so pleasant to relive times when we were inspired by beauty, by mountains, a river, or a forest. We long for similar experiences. In this way, we feed our desire for positive experiences with hopes for the future and memories of the past.

In a sense, all experience is available to us, yet we keep to a narrow path, moving forward to the future or backward to the past. With our minds caught in so narrow a pattern, we see very little of what is actually around us. Our experience flashes by, with new attachments continually leading to disappointment. Our energy leaps from stimulus to stimulus, pulling our consciousness and awareness along with it. Finally, our lives have run their course, and every opportunity for a truly satisfying life has somehow disappeared.

Although there seems to be movement in our lives, in reality our experience is frozen in one dimension. Our minds work very quickly, but in a circular pattern. Even when we try to break out of the circle, every new path seems to end where we began. In attempting to escape, we remain imprisoned in the cycle, blind to the opportunities around us.

Once in this cycle, we are like a closed bud with the richness, color, and perfume locked inside. When we learn to let go, to break out of these patterns of excitement and craving, there is a vast openness, an unrestricted space in which all possibilities await us. But it is not easy to open to new ways, and for many the effort itself can have a grasping quality that only strengthens the enclosing mental pattern.

How do we break this cycle of craving and frustration? One way is to make use of the very habits that established this cycle. For example, we can use memories. Living in the past mostly reinforces these patterns, but at the same time, past experiences often gather deep and heartfelt feelings around them. And these deep feelings can help us to open to all other experiences and situations.

Relax as fully as possible, and let your memories 'float'. Touch lightly on beautiful memories: green valleys, good friends, or happy times with your family. There are times you may remember from early childhood, wonderful times. Experience again your old room, your first friends, your parents when they were young. Look at the images, taste the experience, deepen the feeling until you are enveloped in a warm richness of imagery.

Maintaining the image, imagine that it is in the present, and shift your feelings towards you. Shift them again away from you into the past, and then towards you, back and forth. This shifting can lead you to see experience differently, can lead you to a new perspective. Such a new perspective can help us to understand how our usual way of looking at experience distorts and limits our lives, cutting us off from direct contact with our surroundings and our possibilities. Our perception itself changes. We develop a new quality of seeing, and greater range and depth of feeling.

As our fixed ideas about experience change, we see that up to now we have scarcely appreciated our immediate experience. This lack of attention has reinforced our tendencies to live in the past or to seek new experience in the future. We can change this around. Instead of escaping from each moment in our usual way, we can use our memories as tools to enrich our lives. By visualizing happy experiences, by raising and intensifying feelings such as love and joy, we can transform our negativities. The more deeply we feel our experience, the more we strengthen the positive nature of our lives.

We tend to carefully guard what little experience we have. We are closed, protective. As our experience becomes deeper, we no longer fear losing what we have, and thus no longer need to be defensive. When we overcome our fears, we open naturally to others. We develop trust and remove still more barriers to our ever-deepening experience.

As our experience opens to wider perspectives, our senses, our bodies, and our consciousness become vibrantly alive. Patterns of craving and frustration give way to the flowing interaction with the process of living. All imbalances drop away, and whatever satisfaction or healing we need is provided naturally. This protection, this balance, this genuine self-sufficiency allows us to open to the endless possibility of each moment and to discover the richness and depth of all experience.

Opening to Feeling

Instead of having confidence within ourselves, we constantly look outside ourselves for approval and fulfillment. Even when we are continually disappointed, we keep on searching for and grasping after happiness. We entertain ourselves with parties, drinking, sex, coffee, cigarettes, or whatever, but these pleasures are only temporarily satisfying, like trying to live on spun sugar. Such external pleasures can only lead to an endless cycle of wanting. They are really like poison oak; when we scratch, we relieve the itching sensation temporarily, but the poison ends up spreading over our entire body.

Genuine satisfaction is found only within our hearts, wherein lie peace and a subtle, ecstatic beauty. There, by integrating our body, mind, and senses, we can establish an inner balance and harmony. This inner balance then stays with us in everything we do.

Our problems are in our heads and hearts and the

solutions to our problems are there as well. Our problems arise because we do not let our hearts and heads work well together—it is as if they lived in two different worlds . . . they do not communicate with each other, or meet each other's needs. And when the body and the mind are not sensitive to each other, there can be no real basis for satisfaction.

The bridge between the body and the mind is provided by the senses, some of which are related more closely to the body, some to the mind. Because of this overlap, the senses have the potential to help the body and mind work together naturally. First, however, we must acknowledge our senses and experience them more deeply.

The external pleasures we thought would cultivate our senses have actually dulled them because we have not made full use of them. We usually pass from one experience to another before we know what we are feeling; we are barely able to sense what we experience. We do not give our senses time to develop an experience, or allow our minds and bodies to integrate our feelings.

Our senses are filters through which we perceive our world; when they are dulled, we cannot experience the richness of life, or approach true happiness. In order to touch our senses, we have to contact the feelings of our experience. We need to slow down, to hear and feel the tones and vibrations our feelings are trying to communicate to us; then we can learn how to touch—roughly touch, gently touch. Each sense has physical qualities, but we are often not fully aware of them. We can begin to increase our awareness of our senses by learning to relax and be more open.

Our senses are nourished when we become quiet and relaxed. We can experience each sense, savoring its essence. To do this, touch on one aspect of the senses, and then allow the feeling to go farther. As we go to an even deeper level, we can intensify and enjoy the values and the satisfaction to be found there. As different organisms have different structures, so too the senses. There are various layers in our experience of them; layers to be revealed when we are relaxed, unhurried, and attentive.

Meditation, which encourages us to develop a listening, a live quality, provides us with a way to explore these layers. Using the tools of mindfulness and concentration, we can learn to root out tenseness and let our energy flow through the whole body. Genuine relaxation is more than having a good time or simply resting; it means going beyond the physical form and opening all the senses completely. To experience this is to take a refreshing shower within our heart.

We can encourage this openness and relaxation by visualizing vast, open space, by thinking of all external objects as well as our bodies as being part of this space, all within the immediate moment. Finally, no barriers remain. What is left is a higher awareness, alive and healing, which gives us warmth and nourishment.

We can remain within this space, within this awareness, as long as we like, not needing to focus or hold our

attention on anything. All we need to bring to meditation is ourselves, for our bodies and minds are the foun-
dations of meditation. Breath, which is like a coordinator
of body and mind, is the essence of being that integrates
them.

As we meditate, breathing becomes quiet and regular,
the body relaxes, and the total energy of body and mind
comes alive. This encourages a positive mental attitude,
for when the body and breath are stable, it is easier to
relax the mind and calm the emotions.

It is useful to consider the body as the anchor for the
senses and the mind; they are all interrelated. Feel your
entire physical body. Allow your breathing to become
relaxed and quiet. When your body and breath become
very still, you may feel a very light sensation, almost like
flying, which carries with it a fresh, alive quality. Open all
your cells, even all the molecules that make up your body,
unfolding them like petals. Hold nothing back: open
more than your heart; open your entire body, every atom
of it. Then a beautiful experience can arise that has a
quality you can come back to again and again, a quality
that will heal and sustain you.

Once you touch your inner nature in this way, everything becomes silent. Your body and mind merge in
pure energy; you become truly integrated. Tremendous
benefits flow from that unity, including great joy and
sensitivity. The energy flowing from this openness heals
and nourishes the senses: they fill with sensation, opening
like flowers.

When our minds and bodies become one, we can understand silence and emptiness; we know satisfaction because our lives are balanced. The roots of our tension are cut, so our inner conflict ceases; we become very peaceful and fulfilled.

The more we explore the intensifying of the senses, the more we find a great depth within our feelings. Sensations become richer, textured with subtle nuances, more deeply joyful. We do not have to learn exotic techniques to enrich our lives. Once we contact this heightened feeling within ourselves, it carries us through our daily lives—walking, working, doing any activity. Daily practice means only that we keep on making an effort to continue developing our inner balance as much as we can, wherever we are and whatever we are doing.

Gradually we incorporate this feeling into our thoughts and awareness. It is a kind of spice that gives our lives flavor. Our mind, body, and senses become very alive, as if they possessed a natural intelligence of their own. Even physiological changes can take place. So enjoy this aliveness in which every moment is like a new birth; appreciate it and have confidence.

We can explore the creamy texture of our deeper feelings, and contact an ever subtler level of beauty within our bodies and senses. Within the open space of meditation we can find infinite joy and perfect bliss. We begin to experience a new kind of honesty, a vital energy that comes from real understanding of ourselves, from being genuinely direct and open. This is a dynamic, living process, extending far deeper than externals.

Once we discover this spirit of vitality, which is the essence of awareness, we find that our bodies actually become a channel through which we are capable of contacting a higher level of awareness within ourselves. Although we may still have problems in our lives, we will be fortified against disappointments by our inner joy and strength. We know that our inner beauty and guidance cannot be lost through the actions and attitudes of others. Relying on ourselves through more intimate knowledge of our inner nature is a strong foundation, a real source of nourishment and lasting happiness.

Learning in this way is artistic and beautiful, enabling us to achieve a balance of body and mind, to live in harmony with others, and to bring more meaning into our lives at every level. When we live in this way the results are reflected not only in our own lives, but within the world as well.

Transcending Emotions

Our lives are a continuous flow of one kind of experience after another, with moments of great love and joy often being quickly followed by experiences of anger, frustration, and pain. As this occurs, we tend to categorize our experiences as good or bad, positive or negative. We do not see that by splitting our experience in this way, by treating some experiences as friends and others as enemies, we separate ourselves from the richness of experience as a 'whole'. We become alienated from ourselves, and in the resulting conflict we stimulate energies which create new problems even while we are attempting to solve old ones.

This division of experience creates endless negativities. The more we base our actions on this either-or thinking, the more it becomes our master, making it very difficult for us to find the middle path between the extremes of positive and negative.

The more our energy goes into trying to repress our problems and trying to be happy, the more we reinforce our unhappiness. We thus tend to dwell in a self-perpetuating negativity, a real swamp of confusion. Like a mother dreaming that her child is dying, we experience our suffering almost as if it were more than real. But we can wake up. When we realize that our ideas of good or bad, black or white, are only labels—that existence itself is neutral and only our viewpoint colors it positive or negative—then we know that the real answer lies in ourselves. We have to change our patterns of reacting to experience. For our problems do not lie in what we experience, but in the attitude we have towards it.

When we see how we condition our experience, life itself is both the teaching and the path away from our frustrations. We do not need to change, give up, or lose anything. When we are centered, emotional ups and downs are like the waves on the surface of the ocean— which is calm and peaceful in its depths. Simply by accepting all our emotions as natural, we understand that all experiences have a natural quality, right for the time and place.

We can be grateful for our emotions, for our frustrations, fears, and sorrows; they help us to wake up. We have no clearer messages about what is happening in our lives. Our emotions show us where to direct our attention; rather than obscuring the path, they can clarify and sharpen it. As we penetrate the powerful energies of our emotions, we understand that our obstacles and our spiritual path are one.

When we accept our emotions as they come, we develop an attitude of openness—we can make friends with our emotions and allow them to travel their natural course. Once we adopt this attitude of openness and receptivity, we see everything, in a sense, as perfect.

Any experience is fresh and valuable when we let go of our expectations and resistances, our judgments and conceptualizations. With an attitude of acceptance, even our negative emotions have the potential to increase our energy and strength. We usually see only the negative side of the energy that goes into experiences like anxiety, frustration, anger, and pain, but we can turn these experiences into understanding.

Most of our suffering is psychological, nourished by fear and our identification with the pain. It is important to break down the idea that this is *our* suffering, *our* fear. Concentrate on the feeling, not on thoughts about it. Concentrate on the center of the feeling; penetrate into that space. There is a density of energy in that center that is clear and distinct. This energy has great power, and can transmit great clarity.

Our consciousness can go into the emotion, contacting this pure energy so that our tension breaks. With gentleness and self-understanding we control this energy. Force does not work. So prepare slowly, being careful not to jump suddenly into the midst of negativity. Be calm and sensitive and watch each situation as it arises. With such sensitive meditation, any emotion can be transformed, for emotion *is* this energy . . . we can shape it in different ways. To transform our negativities, we need only learn to touch them skillfully and gently.

Student: When you say accept yourselves as you are, do you mean that we shouldn't try to change?

Rinpoche: We are always rejecting ourselves, blaming ourselves for one thing or another. We may also be accepting negativities in ourselves that are not really there. Instead of rejecting ourselves, it helps to realize that our negativities, true or false, have no solidity. When our thoughts and concepts change, our attitude changes, and a free-floating energy is released. This energy has been blocked by our negativities, which have a fixed quality. The more we loosen our concepts and tightness, the more this energy flows.

Student: When I have a lot of anger and fear, and meditate on it, it becomes infinitely worse.

Rinpoche: Such emotions can become very intense in meditation. Your sense of time can be distorted: one minute can seem like half an hour. There is a certain fear-energy that interferes with and expands certain experiences. And certain meditative states are so highly sensitive that any trouble is compounded.

For example, when you are making every effort to control your thoughts, that is precisely when thoughts become most disturbing. It is not that you have picked a bad time; it is just that the mind becomes very sensitive when we try to work with it. During these times our consciousness is no longer two-, but three-dimensional. When you look through a lens a certain way, everything becomes either larger or smaller. When you are on a certain wavelength, unusual things happen. You may feel blissful or terrible for what may seem like a whole day, when in actuality it is only half an hour.

In meditation, as in life, many things happen, both beautiful and painful. We need to remain aware. Frustration is always close at hand, tempting and playing with us. We must learn to expect it. The sooner our eyes open, the earlier we can counteract any negativities that arise.

Student: Does it help to meditate on our negative emotions, on our anger?

Rinpoche: The antidote to anger is love, compassion, and patience. But until we know how to apply these, we may instead try to force our anger down. We may try this by keeping quiet, by walking, sleeping, reading books —but none of these are antidotes to anger's poison. What we can do is concentrate on the anger, not allowing any other thoughts to enter.

That means we sit with our angry thoughts, focusing our concentration on the anger—not on its object—so that we make no discriminations, have no reactions. Likewise, when anxiety or any other disturbing feeling arises, keep the feeling concentrated. It is important not to lose it. But it is also important not to think further about it or act on it; just feel the energy, nothing more.

This is what I would like you to do. In the morning when you get up, consider all the possibilities which are waiting for you. Be aware and prepared. When your eyes are open, you should be ready for anything. Challenge every minute, for there is always something to be learned. Meditation can help you. If pain, confusion, or sorrow should arise, realize that even such problems can be helpful, like friends talking to you and teasing you. Remember that if you do not play, you do not have any fun. You can play with situations, and see their different aspects; you can respond unexpectedly. This is the way you can challenge each situation. Just let your problems come and don't care so much.

We try to conquer our problems. When we do not react to them, they lose their substance; they are only obstacles when we make them so. When we get caught up in our problems, we are no longer free to choose how we will respond to them. But when we stay unconcerned but aware, we can be championship players. We can play with each happening.

The better we understand our emotions, the sharper, deeper, and clearer our awareness becomes. Finally, we no longer even need to use our conscious minds to free ourselves from our difficulties. On a higher level of being, we do not need to use our brains—only our developed awareness. In order to develop this awareness, we need a path, a map, or instruction, which only our awareness can show us. We can, however, find such a path of awareness within meditation.

When we want to make honey, even though we have the bees and a hive, we still must give the bees time to do their work. Similarly we prepare for meditation through silence and deep relaxation. From this comes awareness.

Student: How can we help someone else who is going through a painful emotional experience?
Rinpoche: Handling intense emotions is not easy; emotions project a form of energy which makes it difficult for anyone near to maintain a balanced perspective. So before we try to help, it is important to know how to sustain a gentle and compassionate attitude. When people are caught up in emotional turmoil, they are very sensitive and vulnerable; they can easily sense underlying emotions and can also easily be hurt by misunderstandings. Therefore, when we want to help, we should be especially mindful of the energy that we ourselves project. Our responsibility is to maintain a sense of awareness that can protect both ourselves and others.

If we are not careful, instead of helping, we may make the emotional imbalance even worse. Emotions, being in substance pure energy, tend to 'soak up' any energy that is directed towards them. It works both ways: while our own energy may stir up the emotion, we may also be 'infected' by the negative energy. The energy seems to intensify itself, as if it had a life of its own.

The ego has a good deal to do with this process. Emotions are defenses set up by the ego to distract attention from itself; under cover of the emotions the ego can then go on about its games and tricks. So when the ego is challenged, the emotions move like mercury to build up a defense.

We therefore must touch the emotions skillfully so that they do not feel the need to fight. We can move behind them gently and can release their energy, transforming them by love and understanding. But unless we are skilled at uncovering the roots of the emotions, even just giving 'emotional support' can be harmful. Emotions fed by emotions and shared with other emotional people, or people susceptible to emotions, can never create a healthy situation.

Student: So what should we do?

Rinpoche: Just allowing the situation to run its natural course and allowing the emotions to run out of steam can be a creative solution. After that, perhaps you could suggest to those involved that they take a deep breath and look at the situation more deeply. This, at times, can be the best and sometimes the only advice or help we should give.

Emotions are rather short-lived among the many elements that make up our existence. Yet at the right time, the comfort of our experience can be a truly valuable gift.

Student: Is it helpful to go to someone else for advice when we are unhappy?

Rinpoche: Attempting to share our emotional problems can just create more problems for both ourselves and others. Instead of running to a friend, try to draw the energy of the problem into your meditation. Let your mind transmute the negativity into a healthy outlook. It is important to be able to stand on your own and face your difficulties directly.

Student: Can you say something about what to do when you are interrupted? When I sit in meditation during the day, if everything is totally quiet, I am calm. Then when my daughter comes in and breaks the calm, I find it very hard to go back to sitting.

Rinpoche: Whenever we are interrupted and get disturbed at the noise, we immediately focus on the object that caused the interruption. Rather than looking at the object, look backward to the experience, and contact that. And again go into your meditation. Let the meditation invite you back. Later on in your practice, even noise is undisturbing because there is no place 'from'. Instead of being an interruption, the noise is merely an interesting happening. Even ordinary occurrences become interesting, because they are a surprise; what did not exist comes into existence.

Student: Rinpoche, when you have a family and little children, almost all your available time is caught up with them. It is difficult to find time to meditate.

Rinpoche: Try to see your children as the meditation. Everything you are involved with in your life—make that your meditation. Meditation does not need a specific place or time. Anyplace, anytime, can become your meditation. This is higher consciousness. Just stay within the situation without any attachment, with no ego involved, with no grasping. Your life will become easy and pleasant, because there will be no room for negativities.

Student: When I am meditating where it's noisy and I find the noise disturbing, wouldn't it be better to go to a quiet place rather than to pretend the noise doesn't disturb me?

Rinpoche: When you understand what is happening, you don't need to find another place. Once we begin to know ourselves and to contact a deeper level of understanding, our relationships with other people and with our environment become balanced and harmonious. Usually, we relate to other people as if they were very foreign to us, like an elephant trying to relate to a peacock or snake. We can change this.

Student: Can you talk about how to get rid of pain?

Rinpoche: Pain can just be accepted; it does not have to bother us, for pain in itself is not bad. That attitude, however, is not acceptable to our common sense; we feel we have to fight with pain, force it to go away. But the only way we can really cure pain is to accept it. That will release the pain itself.

Student: Do you have any ways to help us accept pain?

Rinpoche: We can separate ourselves from it; we can become onlookers watching the part of us that has the pain simply experience it. It is only when we identify with the pain that we are caught up in it.

Student: Can you watch yourself react to the pain?

Rinpoche: Just ask "Who is experiencing the pain?"

Maybe the senses, feelings, habits, or concepts. Put yourself above all of those: just watching, without participating.

Student: Does that make the pain disappear, or doesn't it matter whether it disappears or not?
Rinpoche: Right. It doesn't matter. When our whole attitude becomes different, our consciousness also becomes different. It may be possible for the pain to disappear, but we should take the attitude that it does not matter whether the pain disappears or not. Have no wish for it to disappear. Just watch it.

Student: So if you accept the pain and feel it is all right, then there is nothing to wish for.
Rinpoche: Right. Then fear vanishes too. This is possible for people who have meditated, because they can accept it. It is very difficult for one who has never meditated to accept pain, because the interactions between thoughts, fear, imagination, feelings, and so forth are so strong.

Student: But we have fear because we think we are protecting ourselves.
Rinpoche: As soon as you accept the experience, there is no fear. Accepting involves knowing that there is nothing to protect. We can say that we accept the experience, but acceptance has to go further than the head. Otherwise we continue to identify with pain and fear.

Student: Can we also accept emotions like frustration and anger?

Rinpoche: These emotions are very strong. Normally they have negative effects, but they do have a certain power which is based on awareness. There is very good potential there for someone who knows how to use it. I do not recommend that you arouse anger, hate, or strong emotions. But we should not try to escape or deny them, or suppress them, which we often do.

Student: So if you feel an emotion welling up, let it out, but be aware of what you are doing?

Rinpoche: More than be aware. You have to know how to do it.

Student: How to let it out?

Rinpoche: You have to know how to act. You have to know how to be angry without anger; you have to know how to be attached without attachment. It is not always simple, and it is not just a matter of our awareness. When a person sends up a rocket, he cannot just be aware of what he has done, or just care where it is going. He must know the results exactly; otherwise people will get hurt. There is much responsibility implied in this.

What I am saying is that emotions have value, but only when we know how to use them for spiritual growth and enlightenment. The meditator, by knowing how to use even one emotion, can transcend all emotions. This use of the emotions is part of the expertise by which we can help ourselves and others.

Once we realize that energy appears in different ways, we can embrace the energies of the emotions and bring them into our meditative state. We can learn to relax within these energies when we no longer divide up our experiences into positive and negative. Then the emotions are welcome, because we understand that they are teachings; the emotions themselves can reveal their own meaning, without our needing to look beyond them.

With care, our negative emotions, when mixed with the vitality of meditation, can increase our awareness. It is like going into the sunlight from a darkened room—to be able to see, our eyes must adjust to the light. In a similar way, all our experiences contain dynamism and power, but we must develop our awareness before we can use them well.

Gradually we increase our alertness and awaken our senses: this alertness protects us like a bumper on a car. With more awareness of how our minds function, we begin to free ourselves from our ingrained patterns. This relaxed, yet alert sensitivity allows us to be aware of what is occurring in any situation, therefore freeing us from the manipulation of the emotions.

In this way, we can gradually transform all our negativities, for the more we understand them, the more we see that even they are a part of awareness. Nothing need be ignored or denied. As peacocks can eat even poison, likewise an enlightened person can use all kinds of energy. From the enlightened point of view, there is only one channel: confusion is clear and darkness is bright. This is why Buddhist art portrays both the compassionate and wrathful aspects as manifestations of the same form.

Through insight into the nature of our emotions, life becomes easier. The obstacles that seemed like huge waves to us before, may now seem like only small ripples. We have the ability to choose how we would like to manifest: we can shift freely back and forth; we can be angry, confused, or joyful—whatever we would like to be. This is a genuine creativity, through which we shape our world. In this context, all experience is a part of enlightenment.

We can create a beautiful universe. When our problems become our friends and supporters, like gifts or contributions, we no longer have any problems. Then we have freedom from inner conflict; we have inner peace, the highest freedom there is.

As we begin to enjoy this freedom, our attitude toward ourselves and our experience changes. Our understanding and communication with other people increases, and little by little we can help create an atmosphere of peace and harmony in the world. The more we can free our minds from their either-or tendencies, the more we can experience love and compassion for others. This is a very important step, for openness is the best foundation for spiritual growth. Knowing how to work with all seeming negativities, we can learn how our inner environment works with the nature of our being.

As experience becomes more meaningful, we know how to teach ourselves, how to take care of ourselves.

Knowing that freedom stems from accepting our own nature, our own realization, our own enlightened mind, we can always find the middle way. When we transcend the attachments and aversions of the mind, all seeming negativities become powerful vehicles to enlightenment.

Fascination and Anxiety

The world is a fascinating place, full of beauty, remarkable sensations, all manner of nearly irresistible attractions. But even though these attractions continually occupy our attention, they seldom give us any lasting satisfaction. We are like small birds: our mouths gaping, always hungry. And the hunger seems to go on and on. We are continually unfulfilled, so our dissatisfaction increases even more.

Constantly hungry, we become attracted to what others have; we get caught up in continual searching and grasping, which is an exhausting pursuit. Our minds, tired and distracted, miss the true opportunities for fulfillment. We grasp at the messages our sense perceptions send us and therefore miss the nurturing quality of the natural flow of our own feelings and sensations. Rather than focusing on the sensations we experience, we focus on our thoughts about them—which cannot ever give much satisfaction.

When we become aware of this situation, we can see that it is caused by a subtle psychological progression: the reaching out of fascination leading to anxiety, and dissatisfaction leading to further reaching out. We get caught in this progression because our thoughts, our fascinations, cannot fulfill us; they have no real substance. We cannot hold them. We continually put ourselves in the situation of chasing after rainbows. And the more we chase them, the more anxious and frustrated we become.

We focus our minds on enjoyment and satisfaction, but the way we go about trying to reach these goals has just the opposite effect. Our minds jump from thought to thought—they recall the past, jump to the future, or dwell on some continual attraction. Our minds seldom center on the immediacy of experience, which is where fulfillment lies.

As the flow of mental images persists, our minds continue to produce a seemingly endless flow of thoughts about these images. This is the main factor in establishing our sense of a self which needs to 'have' and needs to 'do'. Even in our meditation when we try not to 'do' anything, the same process keeps on happening.

In meditation, however, this process is so subtle that we often are unaware it is occurring. We may try not to have any expectations or thoughts about our meditation, but they may hide in the back of our minds, manifesting as a type of impatience, a waiting for something to occur. This feeling does not have to be very strong before the unconscious stimulation of expectation—of fascination —flows like a wave into our consciousness. The stronger this feeling is, the 'faster' and more powerful the wave, which has a tense, 'speeded' quality. This leads quickly to the tightness of frustration and anxiety.

At first, our meditation begins to dissolve the sense of self which needs to 'do'. But then the mind chases after images to compensate. Anxiety increases, further aggravating the flow of thoughts and images. And as soon as we become involved with this 'doing' quality, we feel a need for contact—with images, words, concepts, self, or objects. This need grows stronger, and ingrains the patterns even further. It all happens so quickly, that we do not have time to think about it. It is so swift, because of the forceful underlying energy of our expectations and anxiety.

Relaxation can slow down this tense speeded quality. We can relax the mind, slow down our thoughts, create a different 'tone' which loosens our deeper feelings of expectation. When we can slow down and become calm and relaxed, the anxious waves slow down to ripples.

So, in meditation watch your thoughts closely. Simply watch them. Fascination is a rising wave; observe how it appears. It has many sparkling colors, by nature attractive. Good meditators watch the wave grow higher and higher until they understand how fascination causes us to lose the moment. They learn why beautiful images and interesting ideas so easily distract us.

We can learn to alter the cycle of fascination and anxiety by developing awareness of the coming and going of thoughts and images. By expanding each thought and then carrying its feeling to a deeper level, we can avoid succumbing to anxiety—that part of our consciousness that wants to move, to do something.

We can keep ourselves from being swept up into 'doing', into leaving our meditation, by relaxing and maintaining our awareness. When we can keep our balance and be truly still in meditation, no matter what individual thoughts arise, anxiety and fascination lose their power over us, releasing our energy to flow smoothly.

When we free ourselves from the domination of anxiety and fascination, each moment offers us an opportunity to wake up. We can break the patterns that imprison us, and in the energy that is released, we can find the true source of nourishment and satisfaction, the natural freedom of mind.

PART THREE

Reality and Illusion

Reality and Illusion

From an ordinary point of view, the world of our experience is real. It certainly is not an illusion in the sense of a rabbit pulled out of a hat. But along with considering our world as real, we tend to consider much of our world, much of our experience, as permanent. Drawing on this assumption, we build an elaborate ordering of reality using the mutually agreed-upon sets of concepts that explain the nature of our world.

But in truth, all the different aspects of existence are transitory, with each moment a change from the one before. There is nothing in our world that will last for very long. There is no reality to catch hold of, and whatever we try to hold on to will change.

As soon as an experience occurs, it is already past. However, we often only vaguely sense that this process of change is going on—many changes happen so slowly, that they do not seem to happen at all. We often do not see the process, until suddenly we see the result. For example, when we look back upon our childhood, we find that we are not at all—physically or mentally—the same as we were then. Yet we still consider that child as being us.

In order to understand transitoriness more clearly, it is sometimes helpful to think of our lives as being like a dream. When we are dreaming, what we experience seems very real: we spend time with our friends, we hear music, we feel many wonderful sensations. Only when we wake up from the dream do we discover that the experience was not actually 'real'. The field of the mind has provided the stage for all the images, all the action, all the language of the dream. In much the same way, the waking mind supports and orders our passing thoughts, feelings, and perceptions. The result *seems* real and comprises what we know as ordinary experience. However, when we look back on our experience, we see that it is composed of nothing but transitory thoughts and impressions.

Actually realizing that all experience is transitory, that whatever we seek will elude us, can be very frightening, even threatening. Change is upsetting, and the idea of constant change is perhaps more disturbing than we care to think about. We want our world to be at least partially solid and stable, something we can depend upon. We do not see that if any part of our existence were fixed or solid, it would actually pose a great obstacle. For change is what allows growth and development. Transi-

toriness is not a threat at all; it is instead the opening to
new horizons.

There is a story about a frog that lived in a small pond.
Because he had never gone anywhere else, the frog
thought his pond was the whole world. Then one day a
tortoise came to the pond and told the frog that he had
come from the ocean. But the frog had never heard of an
ocean and wondered if it were like his pond. "No," said the
tortoise. "It is much bigger." "Three times bigger?" asked
the frog. The tortoise kept trying to explain to the frog
how big the ocean was, but the frog did not want to hear.
Finally the frog fainted: it was so frightening even to try
to think about such a place.

Like the frog, we often limit our horizons by believing
only what we are familiar with. Though each belief system may express some aspect of truth, they are all based
on ordinary human consciousness and thus can point only
to relative truths, never to anything more. As long as a
belief system belongs to the realm of ideas and concepts,
it limits us to a very small part of the knowledge that is
actually available to us.

Therefore, in order to discover all the possibilities
before us, we must somehow learn to go 'beyond' ordinary human consciousness, and enter the realm of direct
experience. This is difficult to do because our minds only
know how to follow ideas, instructions, and concepts; we
therefore project the idea of going beyond, of transcend-

ing or transmuting. We are still caught up in the idea, and so we remain at our former level of consciousness. As long as we follow our thoughts in this way, we remain at the level of consciousness that is limited to concepts.

Through meditation, we can obtain an understanding of the changing nature of all existence, and can then open to a new way of seeing. Inherent in the realization that our everyday world is actually always changing is the realization of intrinsic awareness. This awareness permeates all seemingly solid form. When we begin to open our perspective and develop this awareness, we discover a vast, unexplored world, a place where each moment brings a fresh kind of experience. It is like learning to swim. When we frantically try to grasp onto something in the water, the water hinders us, but when we relax and float, the water buoys us up. Our dullness, confusion, and restlessness drop away with all other illusions, and our experience takes on new meaning. When we are able to see our world from the perspective of change, we open to a new freedom and awareness.

Obstacles to our progress may still arise, but we can get around them; learning to 'flow' with our experience gives us true stability and freedom. When we discover change as the real nature of existence, our old conception of the world seems dwarfed and limited. Our world comes alive; we are whole again. A new reality emerges from the old, like a phoenix out of fire.

Moving Tapestry of Dreams

Dreams are a reservoir of knowledge and experience, yet they are often overlooked as a vehicle for exploring reality. In the dream state our bodies are at rest, yet we are able to see and hear, move about, and are even able to learn. When we make good use of the dream state, it is almost as if our lives were doubled: instead of a hundred years, we live two hundred.

In early childhood, 'dreamlike' images are a natural part of our lives: we do not force clear distinctions between our dreams and the solid-seeming objects of our waking perceptions. But gradually, as we learn the symbols with which to label our experience, we find that we run into difficulties if we do not follow the conventional ways of looking at experience. We tighten up both physically and mentally. More and more, after our first years of life, interpretation shapes our ways of thinking, both awake and dreaming. We dismiss the dream state as irrelevant to our reality, so in the morning we remember hardly anything of the night before. We gradually lose our sensitivity to the dream state, and then we remember only very special parts of our dreams; most of them are forgotten.

At birth, consciousness is actually very clear, except for the previously existing karmic patterns it contains. This clarity then becomes obscured by the patterns of our waking lives. Gradually, instead of simply dealing with each moment, consciousness collects and then feeds back patterns of images and concepts, and from these the mind creates a sense of separate identity. We seem to have learned, or at least to have accumulated and stored, information, but in actuality, the self is just re-creating and perpetuating itself. This same process occurs in our dream states. Images, concepts, and interpretations are woven into a pattern, one activating the next; our whole life experience is like a moving tapestry.

By defining and judging whatever we experience, our lives become so complex that there is no space, no image without a label. Our underlying clear awareness is totally obscured. It is, however, possible to cut through these obscurations. Interpretations take shape above deeper levels of consciousness, and when we penetrate these externals, we can contact genuinely direct experience— which is without interpretations or categorizations.

Our ordinary tools of consciousness cannot cut through these obscurations because we cling so tightly to the surface level of our experience. We can, however, use the dream state. Although in many ways the dream state is quite similar to the waking state, it has much more flexibility. In dreams we can manipulate images with ease, and by changing dream situations we can learn to change our waking reality. Dreams are not simply fixed patterns of images or collections of reflected images; they are a direct channel to our inner awareness.

Student: Sometimes I am aware that my body is lying in bed, and yet I know I am dreaming. How or why does this happen?

Rinpoche: In the dream state it is possible to see several ways or several dimensions at the same time. While the awakened state is limited by concepts of what is 'real' and 'possible', the sleeping state is more naturally open; it develops patterns spontaneously rather than forcefully. This is why dreams can be important for developing awareness. Realizing, while dreaming, that a dream is a dream can be of great benefit; we can use this knowledge to shape our dreams.

We can even learn to shape our dreams from our awakened state. Advanced yogis are able to do just about anything in their dreams. They can become dragons or mythical birds, become larger or smaller or disappear, go back into childhood and relive experiences, or even fly through space.

At the end of the tenth century there was an Indian master named Atisha, who was invited to Tibet to teach. His students asked how he would do this without know-

ing the language, and he answered that he would manifest to the Tibetans and teach them through their
dreams. Dream language is the same in all cultures.

Usually we compare the awakened state to consciousness and the dream state to unconsciousness. But in
both states we use the same thinking process. The dream
and the waking states aren't so very different from each
other. When we realize that all existence is like a dream,
the gap between sleeping and waking no longer exists.
Experiences we gain from practices we do during our
dream time can then be brought into our daytime experience. For example, we can learn to change the frightening images we see in our dreams into peaceful forms.
Using the same process, we can transmute the negative
emotions we feel during the daytime into increased
awareness. Thus we can use our dream experiences to
develop a more flexible attitude.

Student: I find that my bothersome dreams affect my
whole day. They carry over into the waking state very
strongly.
Rinpoche: The more you understand the nature of
dreams, the less they will bother you. There is really not
so much difference between pleasant and unpleasant. In
a dream I can see a beautiful face or a horrible face.
They are both just expressions; they are both just faces.

On our usual level of understanding we believe there
exists a reality in which we must take a fixed position. But
gradually we can learn to create our own reality. The
world, our reality, is not solid; everything interacts,

everything can be penetrated. There is no single reality. When we realize that situations are not as concrete as we once thought, our seriousness and tenseness towards life begins to dissolve.

It is helpful to think of all our experience as being like a dream. When we do this, then the concepts and self-identities which have boxed us in begin to fall away. As our self-identity becomes less rigid, our problems become lighter. At the same time, a much deeper level of awareness develops.

Student: With practice, at this point it is relatively easy for me to see both the dream state and the waking state as a dream. But whether I'm asleep or awake, I still have a sense of self. Except for a very few times in my life, the knower and the known remain separate and the sense of self remains very rocklike, very hard to penetrate. It is easy to see everything outside me as a dream, but it is still very hard for me to see myself as a dream.

Rinpoche: It is difficult to become free from the hold of the ego. However, once we truly realize that this is all like a dream, the ego changes naturally. We do not need to fight the ego, because we no longer identify with it.

Student: Once we realize this is all a dream, it seems that we could play whatever ego games we chose.

Rinpoche: When we truly have that realization, it is no longer the ego that is acting. We become the energy itself, so that any kind of playing is not personal.

When we are not bound by the restrictions of ego, our

energy is vivid and sharp, like sunshine—so bright that you cannot look at it directly. At that moment, when an emotion arises, it can be expanded until it is larger than our bodies, larger than a mountain, larger than the entire earth and all of space. It becomes so large that it is beyond imagination, beyond mind. The experience is united with the experiencer; this is total expansion, total openness. Penetration takes us beyond thought, beyond substance, beyond action.

Student: Rinpoche, I find the more I meditate, the more I can remember experiences in my dreams.
Rinpoche: This is because in meditation your mind is calm and quiet. Our memories are always with us, and the calmness allows us to see more of them. When we meditate we may think that the mind is empty, but our minds are just more clear than usual. When our minds settle we can see more clearly what is underneath the surface.

Student: Is looking for the beginning of a dream the same as looking for the beginning of a thought?
Rinpoche: Yes, there are similarities. Even when we look closely, it is difficult to find the beginning or the very ending of a dream. The same is true when we try to catch the start of a thought or where the thought ends.

Student: I have a sense of a process occurring when I am asleep or awake. Being awake is like taking one step with your left foot, then being asleep is like taking another with your right foot: day and night. And the dreaming is part of the living.

Rinpoche: We have the same mind, both awake and dreaming.

Student: In waking reality, when I interact with a person, I feel that there is someone there responding. But, in dream reality, is there anyone there?

Rinpoche: There is a text which has a dream dialogue with two people speaking. One says, "If you come to my dream, I will talk to you in the same way as we are talking now." This is actually possible, but I don't want to give you the sense that the dream state and the waking state are exactly the same. I can say such a thing philosophically, and make sense of it intellectually, but practically, we can not say that this state is the same as the waking state.

Student: If I have a dialogue with a friend who has died, am I just dreaming about him, or am I actually communicating with him?

Rinpoche: On the dream level you are communicating. When your friend dies, you take that as real. When you communicate with him in a dream, that also is real—the experience exists. When we pin it down, what is real and what is not real is determined by our experience. Is your dream an experience or not?

Student: But is he also experiencing it?

Rinpoche: We don't know if someone is experiencing the same thing as we are—it's very hard to determine, even when we are awake. He is having an experience, but it is not the same as your experience. I am real; is there anything other than my experience of him?

Student: So then the two realities are one: there is separation in one reality, while in the other reality there is no separation. Is that what you are saying? There is a polarity and there is no polarity.

Rinpoche: To understand the nature of reality needs a great deal of explanation. It can be confusing. What is true for me, may not be true for someone else. However, we all agree upon conventional reality. This is a table. Conceptually, we have no problems accepting that this is a table. We all agree.

Student: If I were to think that perhaps that wasn't a table, would that change everyone else's perception of it?

Rinpoche: As long as we all believe in the table, no.

Student: Does all this mean that if I were perfect in my meditation, then I could see all of my life happening as part of my meditation, day and night, awake and asleep?

Rinpoche: One of the purposes in learning about dreams is to help us realize that the distinctions which we create, such as that between real and unreal, pain and pleasure, have no real foundation. We realize that our total experience is a dream, that a dream is not just what we experience as we sleep at night.

Student: My purpose in looking into these things is to try to stop suffering. How do we stop suffering in waking life?

Do the elements that exist when we are asleep and dreaming also exist when we wake up?

Rinpoche: But the question is, what does awake really mean?

Student: Well, in a simple way it means our eyes are open.

Rinpoche: That is very true, but maybe that is not enough. Consciousness is very much like a dream. A dream is not actually there. Without a foundation or cause, it simply appears. In the same way, even as I experience this appearance, nothing is actually happening.

Student: But consciousness is happening.

Rinpoche: No. Consciousness is like a dream. They are almost the same. We cannot say that they are exactly the same, but a dream is very close to the nature of consciousness. The problem is that we get caught up in making distinctions between the levels of reality of the dream world and the real world. But if we examine them very carefully, we find that the two are very close. During the night, when something appears in a dream, the actual appearing is itself insubstantial. The appearing, the coming, cannot be seen. So the picture, the image, the dream, does not exist. It is nonexistence that we are seeing.

The more deeply this realization becomes established, the more flexible our ability to fully experience life becomes. By more deeply perceiving the nature of dreaming, we can come closer to the reality which is within the dream. We can get to know our dreams so well that we can control them like a television. This knowledge can then be used in our waking reality to change our way of thinking. We can change a dragon into a tiny baby.

Student: But you can't make everyone else believe it.
Rinpoche: No, that is individual reality. We usually cannot see each other's dreams. When we are dreaming, that world is our entire conscious world. At that time we can see how much we can manipulate, refine, and transcend it—how much we can play. Gradually, we realize that, being ourselves a projection, we are as flexible as the other images. So, we can learn to change ourselves as well. Also, as we develop psychically, it is possible that we can share the dreams of our friends.

Student: Last night I dreamed I was standing in a vast field. As I stood there, with no effort at all, I slid down a path that was sandy and gravelly. It was wonderfully delightful. I've never done that.
Rinpoche: The dream which you were projecting is free from the bounds of time or categories of 'real' or 'unreal'. Both the waking state and the sleeping state are like mirrors. You are looking at your face in the mirror, which in this case is the dream. The dream itself has no foundation. It is like a bubble; the image has no seed. Where are the images of last night's dream? Where did they disappear to?

Student: How about the images I perceived yesterday in my apartment; they are gone too. There are apparently two dreams happening—one which we have when we are asleep, and the other which goes on the rest of the time. Are they the same?

Rinpoche: In some ways they are the same; in some ways not. Basically there are two kinds of experience in life: the waking state and the dream state. It is like a point that somehow has two sides. If you want to be convinced that dreaming is no more an illusion than being awake, remember the times when you are dreaming but not sleeping—when you suddenly realize you are somewhere but do not know how you got there. Or you see fantastic images which make you laugh or cry. These images are very similar in both the sleeping and the waking state. Often during the day we get so caught up in dream images that we lose sight of where we are. It is like living in a fiction.

Student: It seems like it all is an illusion, and that is a frightening thought to me.

Rinpoche: What do you mean, frightening?

Student: I mean I'm living in a nonreality now.

Rinpoche: But that means that you are beginning to understand. You may not fully perceive the experience which is happening, but you have a notion, an interpretive notion. Because you are not yet really experiencing, there is fear. But that also is part of the dream.

Student: Is there some way to get rid of that fear?

Rinpoche: That fear is a part of the gap, the separation

we see between the dream and waking reality. But actually, the nature of our entire experience is that of a dream. Let's say that I have a dream about a tiger and a dog and a snake all attacking me, and I am afraid. It is only after I wake up in the morning that I realize that the whole dream program was a part of me. The same thing happens when you become enlightened: at that time you realize that the whole of samsara is a part of your own creation. You are creating all your experience.

When we have dream experiences at night, we can apply what we learn in those dreams to make our lives much easier and healthier. Moving from the dream state to the waking state is like crossing a bridge from one consciousness level to another. With awareness and practice, we can have an entertaining journey.

Student: I can relate to that. But to relate to things like suffering and death as a dream seems somehow wrong. Something in me fights accepting such things as a dream.
Rinpoche: The problem is that you do not respect or really believe in the dream. To some extent you may have developed your awareness of the dream quality of your experience, but you do not yet realize that the dream *is* what you are experiencing. It is not just an idea imposed on the situation.

Student: If I think that death is a part of the dream, then I will not experience the reality of anyone's death, and how it affects me.
Rinpoche: If you actually believe that reality is a dream,

then you would not relate to death from the limited place which tells us that death is a bad thing, suffering, crying . . . Another aspect is that we should not think of the dream as encompassing only external objects. Actually, our entire subjective sense, all our perceptions, all our consciousness—everything—is a dream. The dream is not simply the images of our perception.

Student: If I want to do this practice then, should I be telling myself with a voice in my head?
Rinpoche: No, realize it directly. When you try to force or convince yourself, it will not work.

Student: What is it like when you realize that everything is a dream?
Rinpoche: It is very, very interesting, as well as satisfying.

Student: Is this how you can say samsara is nirvana?
Rinpoche: Yes. That seems very close to the path.

Student: What's it like once you know?
Rinpoche: Even the hardest things become enjoyable and easy. When you realize that everything is like a dream, you attain pure awareness. And the way to attain this awareness is to realize that all experience is like a dream.

Dream Lotus

In dreams we can do the impossible—we can transform our bodies, use telepathy, even fly. Our dream state is like plumbing the depth of the ocean, while our waking state is like sailing on the surface of the sea. Because dreams are not developed consciously, but pop up spontaneously, they bypass the filters present in our waking consciousness. Our dreams can lead us to a knowledge unreachable in our waking state.

However, it is not always easy to work with the dream state, for we still must use our ordinary concepts to make contact with our dream experiences. There are ways, however, to attune ourselves to the density and rhythm of the dream pattern, and thus to tap this source of knowledge. One of these is to practice certain visualizations just before going to sleep.

To encourage this type of visualization, it is best to create the right feeling-tone by deeply relaxing just before sleep. In particular, relax your head and eyes, your neck muscles and back, and finally relax your whole body. Let go of all tension, and, clearing your mind as much as possible, simply lie there and breathe very slowly and softly. Let your mind and body feel the light and soothing quality of relaxation.

Next, lead the mind in the gentle way you might lead a small child. The mind loves feelings very much, so settle it down with warm, joyful, calm feelings. The mind will stop jumping about; your worries and concepts will slip away, and you will be able to deeply relax. Now you can visualize effectively.

When you are feeling very calm and peaceful, visualize a beautiful, soft lotus flower in your throat. The lotus has light-pink petals which curl slightly inwards, and in the center of this lotus there is a luminous red-orange flame which is light at the edges shading to darker at the center. Looking very softly, concentrate on the top of the flame, and continue to visualize it as long as possible.

This flame represents awareness, which has the same luminous quality as the energy in dreams. The experiences of our dream life and our wakeful state have different characteristics. But since their makeup is essentially the same, the awareness of one state can pass unhindered into the other.

Continue to hold the image of the lotus and the flame. As you do so, watch how thoughts arise, and how the visual image of the lotus intertwines with them. Observe how these thoughts and images reflect their past and present associations and their future projections. Watch this process, but continue to concentrate on the lotus, so that your visualization stays clear.

Other images may keep coming into your mind, and you may feel that you cannot keep your mind free from thoughts even for one minute. Do not worry about them, just observe whatever appears. Even though other images and thoughts arise in the mind, as long as the thread of the visualization remains intact, it will carry over into the dream. However, trying to interpret or 'think about' your visualization will break this thread. A gap between the waking and dreaming state is created, and your visualization and your awareness will be lost. Your awareness will be lost in the dream. So, be careful not to force your visualization; just let it happen, but keep your concentration on the lotus.

Let the form reflect into your awareness until your awareness and the image become one. There will then be no room for thought—this is full contemplation. When concentration is complete, subject, consciousness, object, images, all become one.

At first when you pass into the dream state and images arise, you may not remember where they came from. Your awareness, however, will naturally develop until you will be able to see that you are dreaming. When you watch very carefully, you will be able to see the whole creation and evolution of the dream. The dream images, which at first are fuzzy and diffused, will become clear and encompassing.

This clear awareness is like having a special organ of consciousness which can enable us to see from the dream to the waking state. Through this practice, we can see another dimension of experience, and have access to another way of knowing how experience arises. This is important, for when we know this, we can shape our lives. The images which emerge from dream awareness will intensify our waking awareness, allowing us to see more of the nature of existence.

With continuing practice, we scc less and less difference between the waking and the dream state. Our experiences in waking life become more vivid and varied, the result of a lighter and more refined awareness. We are no longer bound by conventional conceptions of time, space, form, and energy. Within this vaster perspective we may also find that the so-called supernatural feats and legends of the great yogis and masters are not myths or miracles. When the consciousness unites the various poles of experience and moves beyond the limits of conventional thought, psychic powers or abilities are actually natural.

This kind of awareness, based on dream practice, can help create an inner balance. Awareness nourishes the mind in a way that nurtures the whole living organism. Awareness illumines previously unseen facets of the mind, and lights the way for us to explore ever-new dimensions of reality.

The Ground of Being

Ordinarily, we see only the surface of our experience. The dust of innumerable concepts and interpretations dulls our senses and perceptions, so that we can see only a small part of what is actually going on. No wonder life so often seems unsatisfactory—we can no longer see its richness.

The mind has a beautiful complexity, but our ordinary perception does not allow us to see it. Our mind is like a laser beam which can penetrate a ream of paper almost instantly . . . yet we see only one hole, even though there are hundreds. Although each layer of our consciousness is touched on by each experience, our awareness is not normally precise enough to allow us to see these levels.

The first stage of experience is what we could call the ground of being. However 'awareness' is a better term for the experience of this level, for at the ground level we do not actually 'experience' anything: our consciousness does not register perceptions as such. At this level there is no difference between the physical and the mental, or between subject and object.

We may experience this ground level occasionally when we are very drunk, or taking drugs; when we are very happy; or when we are at the point of death; when we are badly hurt, or perhaps unconscious from an accident. The ground level appears instantly. There is no preparation for this experience, for at these times there is no sense of time, no sense of past or future. This ground level is like an empty space; there is no specific sense of awareness. The mind seems as if all sense perception were enclosed within what has been described as a black hole—a blackness which is not oppressive, but a kind of openness.

Under most circumstances, the experience of this ground state does not last for long. But while it lasts, it embraces everything; everything functions within it: the mind, consciousness, and all perception. Although the ground state does not have specific qualities, it is the source of all experience, and from it arise all the thoughts and images which comprise our conceptual world.

All of us are part of being; we *are* being. Our total life experience is this being, this ground, which embraces all of existence. Nirvana and samsara are both manifested within this ground level. The more we understand this, the more life becomes rich and fulfilling. We see that this ground of being is totally open; everything is manifest there. Nothing can destroy this openness.

Meditation enables us to remain at this ground state for long periods of time. Because it is a very peaceful state, free from desires and conflicting emotions, some of the Buddha's disciples stayed on this level for hundreds of years. However, this ground level is only an initial stage; nothing can actually be realized there. The mind naturally moves from this ground level to a second stage, which is a more conscious level, similar to recognition. This second stage is not actually sense perception, but rather an intuitive, seeing quality, a lightness and clarity. By very sensitively developing our awareness, we touch this intuitive second level directly.

The first stage of experience is like touching the ground, the second stage is like looking around, and then the third stage occurs, which is like surveying the horizon—observing with more precision and perceptivity. What we usually refer to as 'experience' is produced on the second and third levels. We can learn to recognize these three levels of experience in each thought: first, the ground state; then we recognize the quality of the experience; finally we learn to extend the experience as long as possible.

As we become more familiar with the distinctions and qualities of each of these levels of experience, we are able to appreciate the subtle complexities and the more inward workings of the mind. Until our perception has developed in this way, we are like someone who has never eaten an apricot: we cannot imagine the taste. But once we are skilled at perceiving the arising and flowing of thought, we are able to go beyond this level of perception, to experience a level that is similar to the fresh perception of childhood. We are able to directly experience mind as a process. When we can soar, when we can transmute the quality of the mind, then we approach genuine freedom.

PART FOUR

Beyond Meanings

Dimensions of Meditation

There are many dimensions to the meditative experience. We can have a beautiful experience, very satisfactory and pleasing, but this experience is still limited because it 'belongs' to a 'self'. There is a frame of reference within which we react, and we will, therefore, lose the experience. So we still have our ups and downs. Later our meditative experience may expand and become unlimited: with no point of reference, no center. All and everything is part of the meditation. This may lead into the third stage where there are no distinctions to be made. We wake up and see that reality and truth are not just one dimensional, but jewel-like, with many facets. This level is pure awareness.

Student: At the pure awareness level, you have thoughts, but you are somehow beyond the thoughts?
Rinpoche: You are above the thoughts, in the thoughts,

outside the thoughts. You may still see the thoughts, but you are not involved with them. They have only a small bark—they don't bite very badly.

Student: How can we be aware that we are meditating in this way?

Rinpoche: It is possible to spend many years practicing without making substantial progress. But we can tell when we are meditating well, for on the higher levels of meditation, we are not aware that we are doing anything—there is no reflection. As long as there are walls, as long as there are parameters, we question and try to measure the space. But once we enter into the open space of meditation, we cannot divide it this way or that way. Questions no longer apply.

In beginning meditation it is important to let go of all thoughts, and free ourselves from their past and future. In between we find meditation. But as our meditation becomes more developed, a meditative quality can be discovered intrinsically within each thought and each emotion. Meditation then becomes a natural part of us—an experience which we can carry on throughout our daily lives.

Student: Are you saying that we can use our everyday problems as a basis for meditation?

Rinpoche: Whatever we experience can become our meditation . . . but in our meditation we should not try to sort and select. Our breath, feelings, muscle tension, desires, ego, grasping, and confusion—everything we experience can be our meditation. Meditation is actually a part of us, and we cannot walk away from ourselves.

Meditation not only can help us to solve our problems but can also protect us from their arising. The process of meditation relaxes and calms us so that when any concepts and emotions arise, they no longer draw us into their context. And so their power over us begins to dissolve.

Student: I have the tendency to confuse concentration with tenseness and effort. If I understand what you are saying this is incorrect; I should be more relaxed.
Rinpoche: Meditation is non-rigid concentration. For the beginner, concentration takes effort. But even though there is volition, there should be no force.

Student: What exactly is the ego?
Rinpoche: The ego is closely related to the actions of grasping and identity. But once we learn to meditate, the ego begins to lose its power over us.

Student: My concept of ego equates it with consciousness.
Rinpoche: But that concept is based on certain images or interpretations which arise through your feelings and senses—these are simply patterns without any substantial meaning. The person who can trust his meditation finds there is no name and no form to the experience.

Many people feel that essence and ego are the same. The more deeply you investigate and the more refined your understanding, the stronger your realization that no absolute, no essence or ego exists. These are simply empty words which hold no meaning.

Student: It seems that whenever I meditate my mind is constantly flooded with images.
Rinpoche: Sometimes when concentrating, subconscious images—memories and archetypes—come to the surface. Many unfamiliar experiences sort of pop into consciousness. Some meditation techniques stir and puff up these images. This kind of experience means you are on the path of meditation. Concentration naturally leads to such experiences, but concentration also leads beyond them. Relax, and let go of the 'watcher'. Try not to be aware *of* anything. Use patience. Go back into your meditation and try to stay in touch with the feeling of deep relaxation, and as your meditation experience deepens, your restlessness will naturally subside.

So, do not pay any attention to the quantity or quality of your meditation. Just keep it open. You are the center of your meditation.

Student: Often when I try to concentrate, when I meditate, I get a headache.
Rinpoche: Then your meditation is too rigid or stiff. Forget the concept of meditation; let go of the feeling of ownership. When you have either a good or a bad experience, you feel you are the owner. This holding creates a tightness. When you can let go of the experience, your headaches will disappear. Often we are too careful with

meditation, acting as though we were in a room with a sleeping baby: any noise and baby will wake up. We need to relax and loosen this attitude.

Be kind to your body. Gently massage the neck muscles so that the energy flows freely there. Let go of all your tension and resistances. You do not need to do anything in particular. Your eyes, hands, stomach, bones, and muscles are all taking care of themselves. Let the awareness flow through your body and mind.

Student: But isn't it necessary for someone on the spiritual path to have some kind of guru or personal teacher?
Rinpoche: It is very hard to generalize. Some people may need a guru—others may not. The only way to know is to look within your heart and see whether you can actually manage to progress without your ego or self-delusion getting in the way.

Student: What part *does* religion play in meditation?
Rinpoche: Religion and devotion are useful—they are another aspect of meditation. Religious feeling can be very important, for as soon as you believe and follow, your consciousness follows as well. As long as you believe and have faith and devotion, you will make progress.

Student: Is it just another tool?
Rinpoche: Right. It is not the only way, but it is a very important tool.
Student: Can it become an attachment?
Rinpoche: Yes. You can become attached to gold or to

meditation, to your home or to people. You can be attached to anything. There are no differences: any attachment is still an attachment.

Student: What about philosophy?
Rinpoche: Philosophy is first of all concerned with thoughts and concepts. These thoughts and concepts become refined and then have a direction. This direction comes to a point, which becomes a rule, which becomes a system. This system grows bigger, and gradually an ethical conscience develops—right and wrong, positive and negative, virtue and merit, bad karma—things of that nature. Gradually, then, as philosophy becomes a model, it becomes restricted and tied up with many complex details.

The more questions we ask, the more questions there are. Finally we realize that we do not need to ask questions, for there are no final answers. But if we do not ask the questions to begin with, we may never realize this. In one sense our common knowledge is not useless because it helps us to learn how to give answers . . . but it also shows us that there is no ending to the questions. It is like rubbing two pieces of wood together. They heat up and finally burn themselves out. Intellectual understanding is like that.

The only way not to give answers is to realize finally that there are no answers. Answering is not the answer. Answering contributes to the questioning, and questioning just repeats the cycle. The questions and answers do not lead anywhere; they feed back into each other.

Student: Why did you encourage us to ask questions?
Rinpoche: We have thoughts, so expressing them can help. When we ask questions, we can see where we are. Questioning is one way to know; the other is through experience. When both occur at the same time, that is very good, but sometimes we cannot feel the experience. Eventually it all becomes one and there is no difference.

Questioning and answering will not lead too far, but it can be a useful exercise, not something to reject. When we discard philosophy and intellectual understanding, we shut ourselves off from an important part of ourselves. When we live, study, and work in the world, we need to do this kind of exercise as much as possible. But when we are meditating, there should be no questioning.

When you are confused intellectually, try to feel out the confusion with meditation, work with it. This is not a waste of time—it is all a learning process. When you wake up in the morning, realize this is the time; this is the challenge. Try to learn every instant; your classes are in daily life. You are playing games in this meditation realm twenty-four hours each day. The challenge is, which side is winning, the positive or the negative? What are we getting? In the ultimate sense there is no gain and no loss; but until we realize that truth, we will continue to be involved with gaining and losing. So, for now, we work with what we have.

Thoughts

When we are able to still our body, breath and mind, a very comfortable, soothing feeling naturally arises. As we expand this feeling, we find that we feel very much at home there . . . and we can return to this feeling again and again in daily meditation. We may begin by practicing for just a few minutes each day. Eventually, however, as we extend these periods, we find that we can meditate effortlessly. And through repeated contact with this feeling, our concentration develops naturally. Our progress can be hindered, however, if we try to interpret these feelings intellectually. For the thought process itself separates us from the experience.

Our thoughts are so much a part of us that even when we are meditating we tend to accept the world of ideas and concepts as our reality. We limit ourselves to this familiar realm, and therefore limit our meditation. We see this effect clearly when we closely examine the nature of thoughts.

When a thought arises in the mind, we 'attach' ourselves to it as if it were our child. We feel ourselves as a mother to our thoughts—but this is actually a trick that our minds play on us. In fact, if we watch carefully and try to remain unattached, we can see that each thought arises and passes away without substantial connection to the succeeding one. Thoughts tend to be erratic, to leap from one thing to another, like kangaroos. Each thought has its own character. Some are slow and others fast; one thought may be very positive and the next very negative. Thoughts are just passing through, like cars passing by on the highway. In very rapid succession, one thought comes forth as the last one fades.

As one thought leads to the next, it seems that they have some direction, but despite the sense of motion, there is no genuine progression. Mental events—thoughts —are like a motion picture: though there is a sense of continuity, continuity itself is an illusion created by the projection of a series of similar—but actually individual—images.

As a particular thought or idea arises, it begins to take on form, like a baby growing in the womb. It develops for a while inside us; then it is 'born' as a fully-shaped idea. As soon as the thought emerges, it cries out; we need to take care of it. Thoughts are very difficult and demanding. We need to learn to handle them properly.

By watching our thoughts carefully, we can learn to directly experience each thought or concept as it arises. By gently and skillfully staying with each thought, we can experience the different patterns and tones. This is what is meant by going to the inner experience or by actually becoming the experience.

Concentration is important in order to make contact with the energy within each thought, but forceful concentration is not at all effective. Forcing may seem to work for short periods of time, but new thoughts continue to arise, and concentration falters. We have only half-dealt with one thought when another comes, and then another. To avoid this, it is important to gently guide the mind to a single-pointedness which can be fully concentrated within the inner experience of each thought. Through gentle self-discipline, we can gradually develop and expand this concentration.

When we are very attentive, we can become aware of the space between individual thoughts. This is not easy, so quickly and subtly does one thought fade and the next arise. But there is a rhythm to this process—and when we catch on to this rhythm, we can see a 'gap' between thoughts: a 'space' or a level of consciousness where the senses do not distract us. The space between thoughts has a quality of openness which is very close to emptiness. This space is not caught up with discriminations or obscurations. Reaching it is like diving deep into the ocean; there is a vast stillness. On the surface there may be countless waves, but when we go deep within, there is a profound peace and equilibrium.

This space between thoughts is like the interval between this moment and the future: this thought is gone, but the future one is not yet. In fact, this presence of awareness is not involved with past or future; it is not even involved with our usual idea of the present. Contacting this space is like taking a trip to another world, and the quality of the experience is far different from what we ordinarily meet with.

Once we find this space between thoughts, we can expand it into a deep and full experience. As we expand the calm of the space between thoughts, the mind gradually loses its restlessness, and the natural state of mind begins to reveal itself. At first this state is hard to maintain, because our mind still tends to be distracted by thoughts. But as we develop more balance, our mind gravitates more easily to a deeper level of awareness. When we learn to sustain this awareness for longer and longer periods, it becomes like an internal light, always radiant. This is intrinsic awareness. It frees us from confusion, and from the habitual and seemingly endless sequence of thoughts.

We can expand this calm beyond our bodies, beyond even this world, and can feel the vastness, the centerlessness of open space. Our experience becomes alive, fresh, clear, and positive. The more deeply we enter into this space between thoughts, the more powerful our experience becomes.

Within the space between thoughts we see that mind itself is space, that it is transparent and formless. We see that our thoughts, too, are open and without form. Once we directly experience this sense of open space, we are no longer confined in the boxes of concepts, words, and images that have previously restricted our experience.

In the space between thoughts there is only the crystalline quality of pure awareness. Past and future dissolve, because this space is beyond the realm of concepts . . . vast, open, holding on to nothing, yet permitting everything.

Student: In addition to talking about entering the space between thoughts, you mentioned going into the thought itself. Could you elaborate?

Rinpoche: We can learn to simply keep our awareness in the moment and just be, without creating any separation between our 'self' and the thought. This is the way to cut through or to penetrate a thought. By trying to analyze or grasp a thought, we will always remain outside it. But thoughts are not outside us; reality is not somewhere else.

Thoughts are a little like bubbles rising in the ocean. Within the thought itself is an awareness or clarity, light and fresh. It is important to contact this inner nature of the thought itself.

Student: If I could understand all my thoughts and actions, then . . .

Rinpoche: But that takes someone who is extremely aware. We do not even remember how many thoughts we

had this morning before getting out of bed. Even when
we try to count our thoughts for one hour and see how
many positive, negative, and neutral thoughts we have,
we cannot remember them; we cannot even remember
the thoughts *behind* the thoughts. Only a truly awakened
person can learn to use every single thought to develop
awareness.

Student: Often you say to give up the discriminating
mind, yet the word for wisdom is sometimes translated in
texts as 'discriminating awareness'. Do they mean something different?
Rinpoche: What we call discriminating awareness is very
different from our ordinary discrimination or 'awareness
of' something; it is an intuitive awareness which has a
brighter, higher quality than ordinary awareness. It is a
way of cutting through our dependence on words and
concepts.

This awareness gives us another way of seeing, another
standpoint from which to view experience. Human consciousness can usually see only one or two dimensions
at a time, but with this deeper vision, past, present,
and future unite into one space. All dimensions can be
seen at once.

Student: What does it mean to expand thought? How
can thought itself become meditation?
Rinpoche: First you realize that a thought is coming. Let
your consciousness enter the thought, find its nucleus,
which is a quiet awareness within the thought. That is

seeing. Thought itself is based on awareness: without awareness, there are no thoughts. When you contact that awareness or energy, expand it as much as you can. Make this expansion of the thought an exercise.

Or, look at it this way: one thought is here, the next thought has not yet come; the very moment the present thought is gone, stay in that space before the next comes. That is expanding; thought itself is expanding. Practice in that way. As soon as a concept is gone, that is the place where you stay.

Student: I wonder if you expand that thought and like it so much that you could become attached to it . . . then what?

Rinpoche: Then that is attachment, manifesting as the next thought. When you are liking something, you are holding on; you are stuck there. Therefore, you have this thought. In this way, you are freezing meditation. That is the wrong notion. Let the thoughts go—holding on to them disrupts meditation.

Student: I still don't understand how to stay in the space between thoughts.

Rinpoche: To remain in the space between thoughts, let go of any forcing quality of concentration, and learn how to make no effort. When you can let go of any idea of preparation, even on a very subtle mental level, then you can meditate very naturally, without focusing on any particular form. In this way, your mind actually becomes space; your consciousness and space become one. Awareness is very much like light, and consciousness like space. Without space there can be no light.

The real nature of mind is free from concepts. Even though we talk about a space 'between', this 'between' does not actually exist. There is no specific hole, but in order to point to this experience we use words like 'space' and 'between'. On the surface level, there may be many manifestations, but on a deeper, more subtle level, the mind is totally open and silent.

To contact this silent place, do not put your meditation or your mind in some 'place'. Just be open, with no holding and no center. Once you learn to directly contact this higher level of awareness, then, without needing to oppose them, you will be able to control your thoughts and emotions quite naturally, for they will become completely infused by this awareness. When you are able to surrender your concept-bound mind and enter this open, natural space between thoughts, your higher awareness will function without interruption, and your whole world may be transformed.

Beyond Meanings

When an attempt to find meaning for our lives leads to an interest in the spiritual path, it soon becomes clear that the 'spiritual path' does not mean the same for everyone. What for one is the highest spiritual mindedness is often just the opposite for another. So how do we find the right way? We may turn to philosophy for the answer, but philosophy is often clothed in concepts and theories which we find difficult to relate to our daily lives.

We sometimes forget that theories can be put into practice. Philosophy, because it directs our attention to questions affecting the very core of our lives, is often the doorway to higher realizations. This is why it is important to study the texts of the Buddha's teachings and the philosophical systems that developed from them. These are only external forms, but they are also valuable tools —they give us the means to reach beyond our limitations. We rely on the words because that is how the teachings come to us . . . words point out the directions and stages of the path.

There is always the danger, however, that the external forms will become ends in themselves. Concepts and meanings have such an attraction for our conceptual minds that it is easy to get caught up in them—to get entangled in the words and lose sight of the messages they carry. External forms of any kind, whether that of scholar or that of monk, can be traps: we can easily take up the form and lose the meaning behind it. We can easily mistake the pointing finger for the moon. The spiritual path does not necessarily mean spending a life studying philosophy or talking about spiritual teachings. In order for the spiritual path to have real value for us, we must realize its truths directly.

But how do we apply the highly abstract concepts of the Dharma to our lives? The answer lies in meditation. It is not that we think about these concepts in our meditation; it is rather that, by means of our meditation, we arrive at realizations which help us to integrate the teachings into our lives. We are inspired to study these teachings for further insights and applications. Meditation also uses these same realizations to help us contact an inner awareness which we can use directly. As we learn to tap this awareness, the seeming barrier between meditation and our samsaric minds falls away.

The mind is much more than simply the organ in

which thought arises. For one, mind is the medium of developing meditation. In the broadest sense, the nature of mind *is* meditation. Meditation is the process of working with whatever level of mind we are experiencing.

The deepest level is direct experience. It immediately gives way to the formation of images, and these in turn lead to the interpretation of concepts. This last level of interpretations and concepts is what we usually consider the foundation of our reality, but actually these concepts are 'second hand'—they are far removed from direct experience.

At the level of concepts and ideas, we focus on meanings, sometimes even looking for meanings behind meanings. This searching for meaning is like pursuing words through the dictionary—one word is explained by other words, which are explained by others, and so on. But a meaning is nothing in itself; it has value only in relation to other meanings. Moving from concept to concept, each created by the one before, is a chase which wastes time and energy. Seen in this way, meanings resemble samsara, a word implying the circular motion of a constantly turning wheel. We can never be free until we realize the ultimate uselessness of pursuing this cycle. When we see that we do not have to assign meanings to *anything*, when we allow things to be simply as they are, we discover in them their intrinsic nature.

Since searching for meanings leads only to more meanings, how do we end this cycle? How do we get answers without posing questions? Maybe the answers we are looking for lie beyond concepts, beyond 'answers'. This does not mean that we should stop using words, concepts, and meanings, but only that there is a point at which they are no longer useful.

This is particularly true for when we try to search for meaning in meditation. In fact, when we do find meaning in meditation, something is wrong, because tracking down the meaning of meditation experiences returns us to that useless cycle. When we find meanings, we cannot penetrate beyond them. Looking for meanings leads only to more meanings, even in meditation.

So, during meditation, do not have expectations. Do not try to get anywhere or achieve anything. Fixed goals are just more concepts—they are mental projections, head trips, and lead nowhere. Meditative concentration does not involve such nervous attention. Our meditation should be like listening to a distant empty sound; too much attention only produces tension.

Focusing on specific objectives, reaching for results, prevents real concentration. We get involved again in meanings and evaluations: we concentrate on how well we are following instructions, on whether our meditation is good or bad, clear or confused . . . although all this has nothing to do with meditation itself.

In the beginning, we often confine ourselves to short sessions of formal meditation that we feel are somehow 'special'. This meditation space is limited, like a bird's little nest. We should expand our idea of meditation.

Meditation has no limits; its horizons are as wide as we allow ourselves to see. Once we have learned how to hold our bodies in a balanced way, everything else flows easily —the breathing rhythm natural, the eyes soft and relaxed. This outer form we learn and then forget; it is useful only to promote a calm, relaxed inner state. This outer form then connects us with another deeper level.

Meditative concentration reaches this deeper level. When we go beyond meanings and expectations, we find that the concentrative quality has been there all along. Just letting be is meditation. We can thus sustain this openness and allowingness . . . not only during sitting meditation, but in daily life as well.

As long as we are conscious, we can meditate—there is no particular way we must follow. There are various useful techniques we can employ, but these are all only suggestions, symbols pointing the way. When we reach the heart of meditation, there are no instructions. Meditation is everywhere. Meditation then carries over into daily life, and all that we do is viewed in this same open and relaxed way.

In daily life as in meditation, our basic hindrances are our concepts and expectations. We compartmentalize our lives. We can, however, use this process which interrelates subject and object as our meditation. Every situation—our relationships with the world, with the environment, our friends, our family, our work—can be taken into our meditation.

For example, in the midst of suffering or confusion,

we can stay with the feeling and look at it from every side—after a while the mind seems to soar above our identification with the wanting or the pain. These emotions then lose their immediacy, their sharpness. Meditation does not repress these emotions; it transforms them, allowing the mind to clear. The meditative experience thus provides us insight into another way of viewing experience, allowing us to replace our usual dualistic interpretations with a panoramic vision. Our meditation can then be open . . . a direct experience, unblocked by concepts and interpretations.

When we go beyond our ordinary ways of thinking, we discover a non-conceptual realm, one of pure consciousness. It is beyond the conditional and the conditioned, beyond the ordinary samsaric level. This experience is not derived from the ordinary processing of information received by our senses, nor is it derived from any of the mental activities which constantly contribute 'meaning' to our experience. It is itself immediate experience. In other words, we can free our experiences from the automatic structuring and limiting nature of our concepts, self-images, and attachments. Within each single experience, each perception, is the seed of enlightenment. It is at all times accessible to us.

Experience, then, can become meaning in itself—meaning which reveals itself not in words or concepts, but in the quality of our lives, in the intrinsic beauty and value of all things. When our actions arise naturally from a celebration of living, all concepts drop away. We become meaning itself, enlightened by all existence.

Awareness

As we develop our meditation, gradually our awareness increases. The mind naturally clears of confusions and dissatisfactions, and we touch upon a meditative clarity, an awareness which is there no matter where our thoughts go, no matter what occurs. Once we open to this awareness, we find strength and true confidence in ourselves: not an arrogant confidence, but a positive feeling that is truly integrated and balanced. All our decisions come effortlessly; all our actions arise naturally from this deep and nurturing awareness.

Our usual idea of awareness, however, is bound to an association with objects. The ordinary tendency of the mind is to look ahead, to anticipate and form mental images—a type of awareness that is always object-oriented. This is 'samsaric' awareness—a pattern of anticipating and watching: we watch our concepts, our feelings, our past, our future.

Ordinary awareness is closed and one-dimensional —at this lower level of awareness, our actions, although they may not seem so to us, are remarkably predictable. This is a level of programmed game-playing, where our awareness is constricted within a maze of thoughts and images that continually support the same games and patterns. Only with a quiet mind, an aware mind, can we see these patterns at work and stop them. This is the practice of mindfulness, of being very conscious, every moment, of exactly what is happening in all aspects of our lives.

Mindfulness requires keen observation, but it must be free from interpretation and passing judgment. Practicing mindfulness develops our usual awareness to its most subtle level; with this awareness, we can protect ourselves against being pulled off balance by our thoughts and emotions.

By developing mindfulness, we can go beyond our usual dualistic ways of thinking. We may have an idea of nonduality, but it is not very helpful in taking us beyond dualism, for even the concept of nonduality separates us from the experience. The concept of nonduality thus actually strengthens our dualistic frame of reference. Whatever we ordinarily think or do, we are within an idea, within a thought frame; our awareness is limited. We remain at this level of comprehension until the time comes when we contact a wider awareness that is not concerned with subject or object, an awareness beyond our cognitive understanding. This awareness is the best protection of all; through it our whole being protects itself naturally.

Underneath the surface level of games is a clear and beautiful awareness, an awareness which is not *of* anything, but is total openness. However, to go beyond the idea to the experience itself is a difficult jump. The first obstacle is the subjective orientation of the mind—the observer, the independent watcher. We seldom transcend this part of our ego-mind, because it is the observer that gives us the sense of our being 'real'. Even in our meditation, we are held back by this sense of identity, the conceptual part of our minds that says "this is me," that "does" the meditation, that "has" an experience.

When we seek or emphasize meditation experiences, we stir up a grasping quality which brings our samsaric mind into the meditation itself. We attach meanings to an insight, destroying it by turning it into an object within a dualistic framework. By trying to hold onto the experience, we cut it off.

Even the high, blissful feelings that we may have in meditation, though they can be positive and opening, easily become hindrances when we come to view them as 'objectives' of our meditation. When that occurs, we tend to skip over the totality of the experience, breaking it down into details which our minds feel familiar with. We center on the image, the colors, the emotional highs. But these manifestations are only the illusory backwash, the 'fallout' of the experience. Eventually we realize that when we lock our vision on to the familiar forms of our samsaric world, whatever we encounter or achieve can only repeat our former experiences. We are cutting ourselves off from anything larger, deeper, more open.

It is helpful to remember that the awareness we seek will ultimately come; all we have to do is to stop holding on, and let even the beautiful experiences pass on. Do not think about them; do not expect anything. Just let them be—watch them arise, manifest, and fade. Your level of concentration will deepen as your need to grasp and discriminate dies away.

There are several exercises that will aid in increasing awareness. These techniques, however, are only tools. They help to make possible certain experiences, but the experiences do not depend on the techniques. The techniques work because the experiences are already with us, always accessible.

Whenever a thought arises, we usually feel the need to label and identify it. Try to stop this process. Although you can feel the thought, see it, and experience it happening, the thought itself is a projection of the 'watcher'. The thought is not separate from the 'watcher'.

To understand this, simply watch the flow of mental images pass through your mind. As past and future image-projections pass by, cut between them, not by looking at the thoughts and images, but by looking at 'who' is watching the thoughts. Try to develop a feeling for the thoughts watching the 'watcher'.

When you face the 'watcher' directly, your awareness and the 'watcher' become one. There is no self to watch anything. There is only watching, only the process. There is no subject and object. The process is the experience . . . or, you could say, pure awareness.

Observing the mind carefully shows that the mind manifests our objects of experience directly. Subject and object occur in the mind simultaneously, and both are manifestations of the mind. There is no position to stand on, nothing to investigate. There is nothing to look back on or forward to.

Having no position, no identity, nothing to relate to, may seem very frightening—but to be frightened we need to have something to be frightened of. At the particular moment we reach this state of having 'no position', we no longer are under the ego's sway; our bodies and minds are totally open and receptive. Danger can come only when two things clash. But in this moment of pure awareness, beyond dualism, there is no longer division into subject and object; there can be no enemy; there can be nothing to fear.

But how can we exist without the props of our concepts? How can such an existence have any meaning for us? It is hard at first to accept that we can exist without thoughts. Yet we can begin to see this possibility when in our meditation we learn to contact a silent state in between our thoughts. We can look into this needle eye; this is the space to concentrate on. The very instant one thought fades, catch the energy of the seeing quality in that space. Just stay in that energy between the past and the future.

A word of caution can avoid confusion. We can call this moment between past and future the present, but in doing so we are only pointing. In truth, the present does not exist, because the present is always the product of the consciousness being aware *of* something. The same can be said about the concept of time. Through conceptualizing and interpreting our experience, we create the idea of time. We need this sense of time in order to have experience. When we unite the subject and the object of experience we go beyond 'being aware of'; we transcend our ordinary mind. We are then no longer caught in time, identity, or its associations.

Letting go of all thoughts and images, letting them go wherever they will, reveals there is nothing behind, no independent watcher, no teacher observing his pupils at work. There is no commentator reporting and judging behind the thoughts. There is nothing at all 'behind', not even a 'me' . . . only an immediate, genuine present. In other words, there is no flow of time, no past, present, or future. Everything is in the moment.

When images come into your mind, bypass them. Stay with the energy, the seeingness quality, of the thought itself. Gradually feel out an opening which is part of the thought, an empty place. See this opening, and expand it. In this 'seeing' time it is important also to listen. When we see in this way, we feel as though we were hearing with our eyes; the seeing quality becomes a hearing quality when we keep the eyes loose and relaxed. Now stay in that place. At the instant that thoughts and concepts come, try to see their quality of aliveness.

Every single thought has a nucleus of energy, a center of power and awareness that we can easily find once we put aside the ideas of doing or achieving. The energy in the center just opens itself. This is being. Being needs no improvements; it needs no doing or moving. Being is not past, not future, not even present. Yet we can expand this state of awareness. First find the small gaps, the little points of entry you will learn to recognize. Then make these gaps bigger, until they expand into the whole. At first you will find you are watching, relating to the situation. Later you can engage the total body, and mind; everything becomes a part of the awareness. You can expand it beyond your body, beyond the room. There are no limits to it. You are one with your experience. That is the meditation practice: expanding, contracting, and expanding again this state of awareness.

This pristine awareness belongs to nothing whatsoever, not to us, not to any place or any time. No one owns it. It is completely open, a new dimension. This universal level of awareness includes everything—individual consciousness embraces all consciousness. Nothing is rejected or excluded; everything is clear. We become very clear, totally balanced.

As this intrinsic awareness is expanded, we find that we act harmoniously in each life situation. No longer hampered by conceptions of how things should be, we can be effective in undreamed-of ways. Being in unity with each situation, we respond in total harmony. Our awareness has a dynamic quality, balancing us in a way which allows our energies to flow freely and smoothly. In this relaxed, meditative state we enter into the full richness and depth of experience. This is the beauty and the potential of being.

The Illusion of Now

Much is said these days about the importance of living in the present, about the importance of 'here' and 'now'. But is there actually any 'now'? When we very carefully look at just what 'now' is, we may conclude that it does not exist. We may see that there is no 'present'.

At first this seems absurd: I have thoughts *now*, and they happen to me *here*. Whatever experience is happening is obviously happening *now*. I am here; you are there. I can talk to you; you can talk to me. There is no question that we both consider each other real. This is all very simple.

Yet the reality is different for each of us. From my point of view I see one thing, from yours you see another. From my viewpoint, I am the subject of the experience and you are the object. For you, of course, this is reversed.

Neither of us experiences exactly the same reality. Even if we attempt to duplicate, absolutely precisely, the circumstances of a specific experience, it would never be exactly the same. Even if we could 'give' someone else our experience, the experience would not be the same for him, for he would see it from his own perspective. Our experiences, our realities, depend on our individual consciousness. And just how stable is that consciousness? Drugs, disease, fever, heat, fatigue, all can profoundly affect our minds. We can see dragons, or colored patterns, or the room moving. We know that *these* experiences are not real . . . but what *is* real?

Our sensations, perceptions, thoughts, recognitions, memories, experiences, feelings, concepts, emotions: all are formed into a pattern, just as the structure of a flower is a pattern. When we take a flower apart to see how it is made, it is no longer a flower. Similarly, when we separate our experience into its 'parts', it is no longer the same experience.

Our ordinary experience falls into a dualistic pattern: we divide the world into the experiencer (I, the subject) and what is experienced (it, the object). As soon as we have a particular experience, the I (the subject) thinks about or in some way considers the experience (the object). But our thoughts are only reflections of the experience, they cannot be the experience itself. Rather than being single 'frames' of experience, our experiences are superimposed upon each other.

By attempting to classify and to sort experience, we

create only a confusion of layers and divisions. We may blame this confusion on the complexities of modern life. So we try to simplify our lives by giving up our responsibilities in order to live in the 'present'. But this living in the 'present' still turns out to be a grasping at experience, still a subject examining an object.

Our very ideas about what it means to be in the 'present', or to be here 'now', take root and entangle us with their complexities. Where is this mind, my mind in which I believe that the ideas and experiences occur? Thoughts exist; we have a sense of the present; we have consciousness. But when we try to pinpoint the actual experience we are having, we cannot find anything in our description of the experience that is actually real. What we do find is never the actuality of experience, but only some set of concepts we have formed about our experience. When we try to live in the 'present', we set out to go beyond concepts, beyond time, beyond our usual experiences, but all we do in our earnest anticipation is reinforce our dualistic mind.

So how is it possible to go beyond this surface, or relative realm, when even the desire to go beyond it turns out to prevent us from doing so? The first step is to realize that all things belonging to the relative realm, including language, ideas, and concepts, are forms like clouds in the sky. They look solid; they have different shapes; they move about; yet they are not so different from the sky they float in. In the same way, we make forms out of our different experiences by means of our emotions, our images, and our concepts. We develop 'story lines' which resemble the cloud dragons that writhe across the sky. We usually regard these 'cloud' experiences as if they were real objects, separate from us. But when we understand that they are surface manifestations, we can relax and contact the subtle space beyond the 'cloud-like' concepts and 'cloud-like' emotions, the space where there is no duality of subject and object.

At first it is difficult to accept that this empty space exists. Because we have not developed the kind of perception that is required, we have difficulty understanding the experience. So we first need to gain an intellectual understanding; then we can open ourselves to the actual experience through meditation. In the one instance the intellectual understanding supports the experience; in the other, the experience inspires a deeper understanding. They deepen together, in mutual support.

Our intellectual understanding is a testing mechanism, one which develops a means of proving things in a logical way. This is an important faculty—but at a certain point it becomes less and less dependable, because concepts and logic take us only so far. Only experience can take us beyond images, beyond concepts and words, beyond time. But this is not our usual idea of experience . . . it is pure awareness.

Meditation helps us to let our concepts and ideas yield to this open awareness. In meditation we make our closest contact with our experiential side, where enlightenment, higher consciousness, is found. When we pass directly into any moment, when we dissolve the forms or 'clouds' of concepts and yield to pure experience, we discover our great resource, enlightened space. We can mine our experience to find this great treasure which lies within every thought.

Once this understanding arises, everything is a part of meditation. We are centered in the immediacy of experience, and yet still participating in its outward forms, using concepts, gestures, and so on, to manifest our inner experience. This understanding is true integration, a genuine connection of our whole being with the reality of experience, with the 'now' which is unlimited by time or space.

It is possible to discover this 'reality', this 'now', during meditation. We find it in the space both in and between thoughts: this space is a still, quiet 'ground', which is the basis of consciousness. This 'ground' is totally receptive; all information from our senses settles there, like seeds strewn in a field. These 'seeds' include all experiences and all mental action, positive or negative; all are planted in this 'ground'. When conditions are right, the 'seeds' sprout. This sprouting, this springing to life, is the working out of karma. The 'ground' for each of us is the same. Karma then, is the impulse which transforms this ground-consciousness into the unique consciousness of each individual, giving rise to the individualized consciousness of samsara.

Consciousness, taken by itself, has no determining characteristics. We can say that this is its 'nirvanic' aspect. Yet we can say the same for 'samsaric' consciousness . . . the only difference is that in the samsaric realm, thoughts create a dualism, a sense of subject and object and a sense of separation between them.

Our usual 'now' discriminates between a 'this' presence of nowness and a 'that' presence of nowness. So before we can actually experience the 'presence of awareness', it is necessary to transcend these concepts and this process of discrimination. Until then we can never be sure whether our consciousness is disclosing reality or illusion.

There is a story about a cowherd who wished to learn how to meditate. He was, however, having difficulties, because he had spent his whole life tending cows and knew only the ways of the animals in the fields. One day his teacher, Nagarjuna, asked him how his meditation practice was progressing. The cowherd replied that whenever he tried to meditate, the faces of his cows kept entering his mind. Then Nagarjuna asked, "Can you think even more vividly about what you see? Would you practice this visualization for six months?" The man replied that he would.

Every day, for eight hours, the cowherd concentrated intently on visualizing a cow's face. After six months, the man's face became just like a cow's. He even grew horns! When Nagarjuna returned and told the cowherd that it was time to leave his cottage, the man replied that he could not, because his horns were too big to pass through the door. So Nagarjuna told him to meditate again in the same way, but to visualize a cow without horns. After a few days, the horns disappeared, and the man was able to leave his cottage. At this point, Nagarjuna felt the cowherd was ready to receive the higher teachings.

This is the way consciousness works. It can create an illusion and turn the world into samsara. Yet the same consciousness can pierce the illusion and the world is realized as nirvana. The means for doing either lies completely within us, and the choice is ours alone.

PART FIVE

The Living Dharma

The Dharma Within

For many lifetimes we have ignored our potential for awakening and have followed instead our ego's demands. There is a time, however, when it becomes clear that our selfish pursuits have led us only to boredom, anxiety, and frustration. We then may begin to look for more lasting satisfaction, and this search may lead us to the Dharma, the Buddha's teachings.

However, our initial interest in the teaching often has a selfish side. We may hope that we can somehow relieve our boredom and frustration by taking part in an 'exotic' way of life, or we may look to the Dharma to solve all our problems, to make us happy and to free us from confusion and depression. So we are often disappointed when our lives do not suddenly become blissful and fulfilled.

Because we have innumerable expectations of the Dharma, it is easy to lose interest when there are no immediate results . . . we discover that it takes effort to persevere on the path to enlightenment. We are easily lured from our search by friends, by family, and by our own desires. It is easy to get caught between our desires for enjoyment and our attempts to follow the teachings and to strengthen our practice. For this reason, once we find a teaching which can help us, it is important that we stay with it, that we immerse ourselves in the Dharma as much as we can. By doing this we realize the true nature of the teachings, and find that the Dharma is a way of life in which selfish desires have no meaning or attraction.

At one time the Buddha instructed his cousin, Nanda, to study and practice the Dharma more deeply, but Nanda refused, saying that he had no time. "I want to be with the woman I love. Besides, I don't like study or discipline." So the Buddha replied, "Well, then, come take a short journey with me; there is a place I would like you to see."

Nanda agreed to the trip so long as they were not gone too long. And so the Buddha proceeded to fly Nanda to one of the heavenly realms. He then left his cousin to look around, while he himself went to meditate in a nearby grove.

Everywhere Nanda looked were palaces glistening with iridescent lights. Princely men accompanied by lovely ladies were wandering here and there, dancing, listening to teachings, and walking in pleasure gardens where minstrels played. When Nanda looked up, he saw heavenly maidens flying through the air. He was so astounded by the beauty of the place that he did not notice that many hours had passed. But he did notice that, while everyone else had a companion, he was alone, watching from the outside. Then he noticed five maidens, more beautiful than all the rest combined, entering a palace. There were no men in sight, so he went up to them and said, "You are the only single women I have seen. I am curious; who are you?" And they replied, "Oh, we are waiting for a certain youth who is becoming interested in practicing the Dharma. Because he is creating positive karma, he will be born here." "Who is that lucky man?" he asked. "Buddha's cousin," they replied. Nanda was so elated by their answer that he hurried back to where the Buddha was meditating and asked to be accepted as a student.

Like us, at first Nanda was not attracted to the Dharma itself; his interest was in what could make his life more enjoyable. Later, however, as he developed his practice, he discovered that the depth and beauty of the Dharma surpassed the glory of the heavenly realms. Having transmuted his worldly attachments, he became enlightened.

To practice the Dharma is more difficult for us, because we live in more difficult times. Today, as everyone struggles for enjoyment, money, power, or position, there is much to distract us. To follow the Dharma takes patience, effort, and discipline; it takes time to develop understanding and skill in meditation. Even when we have the motivation to practice, we may not have the time or the opportunity. Or we may not find a teacher we can trust. There remain some true teachers in this dark age of the Kali Yuga, but there are many others who can waste our time. They may give us what we think are very impressive teachings or even powers, but these may be of no real value in the end.

There is a story about a man who herded goats for a living. His work was strenuous, and it always seemed to him that he never had enough to eat, so he got into the habit of stealing the goats' milk before he took the animals home to be milked by their owner. He always made sure to take more than enough, so that he would not be hungry later. Every day he milked the goats, drank what he could, and threw the remainder into the river that flowed by the cave where he took shelter.

Now there was a family of Nagas who lived in the river, and Nagas love goat's milk. The king of the Nagas thought that whoever would offer so much precious milk must be doing so for a reason, so he appeared one evening to the goatherd and asked, "For what reason do you offer us this wonderful food?" Said the goatherd, "I am a very great man; therefore, I feed you." The Naga replied, "Dear master, what then can I offer you? I can give you whatever powers you would like." The goatherd, elated, said, "I would like to be able to sit in midair; I will then attract many disciples due to my ability." The Naga replied, "Fine. I will arrange this for you if you will continue to supply me with goat's milk. Whenever you give teachings you may sit on my back, but I shall remain invisible to everyone else."

Word spread of the goatherd's ability to sit in midair, and many villagers came to receive teachings from him. Although his teachings made little sense, many people worshiped him because of his 'power'.

When the great Pandit Nagarjuna heard about this goatherd, he came to see him. The Naga, realizing that such an accomplished master as Nagarjuna would be able to see him, quickly ran away, leaving the goatherd to tumble to the ground. Disillusioned and disgusted, all the disciples went away.

Like the goatherd, we may seem for a time to gain certain powers or abilities, but power that comes from someone else cannot be relied upon. The real power is the ability to control our minds and emotions, and this can be achieved only by means of our own efforts.

Because the real experience of enlightenment can come only through our own actions, we must make whatever we do contribute to our growth. Even ordinary activities, such as working in the kitchen or in a factory, offer an opportunity to develop our awareness and our willingness to serve others. There is never a lack of opportunity to test ourselves, to face ourselves, to be honest and sincere. True devotion, trust, and acceptance begin in our own hearts. Later, when we must face difficult situations, we will not forget the teachings of our inner understanding; these difficulties will turn into new opportunities to grow and to awaken inwardly.

There once was a young monk named Paka Trubang-wa. He did not know how to read, so his teacher told him to spend his days cleaning the temple. Instead of studying the texts, he spent years cleaning and cleaning and cleaning. He was told that as he cleaned, he was to repeat, "The dust is gone; the smell is gone." One day he thought, "What is dust?" At that moment he understood that the real dust is our fettering emotions. The more he repeated the words, the more he realized the nature of existence.

It is our motivation, our concentration, our mindfulness that is important; we can transmute whatever we do, turning the dust into gold. In most cases, if someone were to tell us to do nothing but clean a temple, we would feel resentment. But when we accept all aspects of life, we find that we can learn from any situation. The Dharma actually becomes a part of us, and we become a part of the Dharma. Strength comes, and encouragement and confidence follow.

The eighteenth-century Tibetan lama Jigmay Lingpa once said, "Although you may have acquired great knowledge and wisdom through years of study and practice, and although you may have learned to be patient and to vigorously practice meditation, still you may be far from attaining enlightenment. One can attain the ultimate realization only through sincere devotion and total trust in the teachings and the teacher."

Trust and devotion, when combined with an awareness of the responsibility we have to others, lead into true compassion for all living beings, and therefore to enlightenment. Devotion and compassion complement each other and support our practice. When our compassion is strong enough, it inspires our devotion; and when we have both devotion and compassion—a loving openness for all sentient life—there is balance and harmony.

It is very simple. Devotion and compassion can take us very close to absolute reality. Devotion opens the heart, where our essential energy or awareness resides, manifesting itself as our inner guidance. Devotion means surrendering to this higher energy, this pure awareness. Surrender requires openness, allowing the Dharma to reach our hearts. Compassion provides the door.

Once we can open ourselves, all dualistic concepts dissolve like clouds. We accept every part of our experience, because everything is seen as appropriate and harmonious. We may still have to face many obstacles, but we learn to accept our shortcomings with gentleness. Once we learn to open ourselves through the Dharma, we find the Dharma is itself our trustworthy guide, our ever-present friend and companion. By opening, we recognize the Buddha's teachings in all of our experience.

Everything is then part of the Dharma. When the Dharma enters our minds, our hearts, and our feelings, and flows through our bloodstream, we are the living Dharma. This understanding is the Dharma within; there are no walls between us and the Dharma. This, we discover, is a surrendering to our own true nature.

Refuge

The first and most fundamental step on the Buddhist path is to take refuge in the Buddha, the Dharma, and the Sangha, the Spiritual Assembly. This indicates that we accept these Three Jewels as our true guides and protectors along the path to enlightenment.

We take refuge in our own teacher as a manifestation of the Buddha. We take refuge in the Dharma, in the teachings as represented by the writings and commentaries in the Buddhist canon. We take refuge in the Sangha, our fellow-travelers on the path—past, present, and future—whose own practice and efforts continually encourage us.

It is natural to begin by following what we believe to be spiritually higher than we are. In most ways this is good; we learn how to place less emphasis on our own desires, how to respect the needs of others, how to be faithful.

But we can only learn so much from teachers and from books; finally, we need to open to our own understanding, to realize spiritual truths from our inner experience. When we genuinely open, then we establish our inner relationship to the Buddha, the Dharma, and the Sangha. We begin to wake up to enlightenment.

'Spiritual' actions are those which happen naturally when we act with an open heart. Yet the teachings only point the way to this openness, and it is not easy to travel to where the teachings point. Many learn to 'act' in accordance with the teachings; not so many learn to actually live them.

For instance, the teachings say to give up the ego. We may perhaps try giving up our 'self-interest' by joining a spiritual group, or by spending our time studying scriptures. But the ego is as much at home in a library or even a monastery as it is in a movie theater—maybe even more so. There are many who are very proud of their knowledge, of their visualizations, meditations, initiations, sadhanas, mandalas. And there are even those who are proud of their religious experiences.

Enlightenment, however, has nothing to do with concepts or acquisitions. The real giving up of ego occurs when we see that there is no difference between 'inner' and 'outer', when we find the wisdom of the Buddha within ourselves. On our samsaric level, we may suppose that the Buddha discovered some extraordinary wisdom which we can glean from the teachings he left behind. But Buddhadharma is not that kind of teaching. What the Buddha realized centuries ago is within consciousness itself; there is nothing in his realization which belonged to him. The enlightenment quality is always there, always accessible.

Some might say that looking inside ourselves for spiritual truths is egocentric and selfish, and that egolessness and selflessness lie in working for others in the world. But until we find our inner truth, our work in the world will always revolve around our 'selves'. As long as we think about the world in terms of 'self' and 'others', our actions will be selfish. Our 'self' follows us wherever we go, so positive results will be limited.

Before we can help others, we need to find as much strength within ourselves as we can. We can find this strength by allowing the Buddha and Dharma to come alive within us. Most of us, however, are not yet able to experience this inner truth. We may try, but for now it seems we must live on the more superficial, subject-object oriented level.

This is why meditation is so important. In meditation we may have experiential realizations which break through our conceptual way of dealing with experiences, and these realizations help us to see from a more enlightened point of view. We contact the calmness and clarity which lie below the conceptual level. Meditation is then our refuge, for we can call on it whenever we need it to give us balance. Taking refuge in ourselves in this way gives us a stronger basis and greater confidence to cope with everyday life. This is refuge at a higher level.

The ultimate refuge lies in a steady contact with the meditative state within which we discover the immediacy of Being, in which no artificial distinctions exist. On this highest level, we see all experience as the pure awareness which we reach through meditation. There is no Buddha, no Dharma, no Sangha. There is no subject or object, no 'I' to take refuge in anything; the concept of taking refuge drops away.

Once we know how to take refuge, and once we understand that there is no concept of an 'I' that needs to be reinforced, we have true protection. As soon as we realize that the Buddha, Dharma, and Sangha arc living rcalitics, which is to say that all experience is part of the Buddha, Dharma, and Sangha, the religious experience is a part of us. Experience is then on a plane entirely different from the ordinary level of sensations and perceptions. Seeing, hearing, feeling, touching: all dimensions of experience are fully alive, infinitely rich.

The source for learning and for studying the Dharma is always at hand; we do not have to go out and buy a copy of it, for it is always present in our experience. This living Dharma is the teaching. When we open to it, when we contact that living experience, the meaning of the Sangha, too, will open. We will see the essential unity of all beings. As soon as we have integrated our experience, the Buddha himself will appear. So every day we should remind ourselves of the living Buddha, Dharma, and Sangha; this is taking refuge.

There are, then, various levels of taking refuge, depending on our understanding. In the beginning we realize that the Buddha, Dharma, and Sangha can guide and support us, nourish and comfort us. At this point we are concerned with taking care of ourselves and making ourselves healthy in body and mind. On a somewhat deeper level we realize that the Buddhadharma is the center of our lives, that there is beauty and meaning in all experience. On a still deeper level we realize the Buddha, Dharma, and Sangha are always within us, so there is no need for external worship. On the most profound level, there is no longer any refuge, because the ego no longer exists. There is only a mandala—perfect in all dimensions.

Love and Compassion

Deepening our understanding of existence opens the door to compassion. Developing awareness of the pain and ignorance which we, as well as all others, experience stimulates sympathy, then empathy. This developing concern for others inspires a feeling of love; a love that loses its connections to our concepts and senses, a love that is without subject or object.

Compassion is the ability to fully experience someone else's situation. Close family relationships help to develop this ability, but these days the sense of family unity is not strong. Without the support of the family, we tend to draw inside ourselves. Since we find it so hard to relate to others, even our good friends, we devote our efforts to protecting ourselves and our possessions. Our concern seldom goes beyond ourselves, beyond our personal needs and desires. Caring for and responsiveness to others, both basic to compassion, have little chance to grow.

One way to learn compassion is to cultivate the *wish*

to help others. This simple gesture automatically opens the heart. We broaden our perspectives and increase our sensitivity to the needs of others, and this then leads us to develop the ability to be of actual help. Eventually we can learn to love without any ulterior motive or sense of self. This feeling of selfless love stimulates an openness that allows compassion to arise naturally. We can then act with skill and compassion in all circumstances.

Student: But how do we do this, how do we learn to put aside our self-centeredness?
Rinpoche: Openness ultimately means compassion. The more open you let yourself be, the more you will be able to communicate with friends, with family, with anyone. Rather than suppressing or trying to avoid your feelings, as much as you can open your heart, your feelings, your whole personality. Open to your deeper levels of feeling. You can do this by relaxation, the key to meditation.

Be very still, breathe very softly and gently, and keep your mind in the presence of awareness. Once relaxation is established in this way, it will heal your inner feelings. Then inner warmth will come. With this inner warmth and inner relaxation you will feel more openness, and with this openness, more communication. Because inner warmth transforms as wisdom, you will be able to see other people's situations more clearly, and with this clarity, you can learn more about yourself as well. You can open to your inner nature.

When your heart truly opens, you can communicate

with all beings, with all existence. You can see the nature of samsara. Openness is the key to compassion, so once you can develop more openness, ego and self-grasping lose their hold. With less self-centeredness you can see that each individual must go through this cycle of samsara. You learn more acceptance, and compassion grows deeper and more encompassing.

Genuine compassion is beyond thoughts, beyond self, free from all belief that there is an 'I' involved in the act of compassion. True compassion, therefore, generates a deep sense of acceptance and even forgiveness towards those who have caused us pain or unhappiness. When we are sensitive to weaknesses and selfishness in others, we realize that the harm they do is done simply out of ignorance.

Student: I have trouble accepting what you are saying about forgiveness when I think of all the people who suffered and died during World War II.
Rinpoche: It is actually healing to develop compassion for those who do terrible things. The actions of such people show that they have no true awareness of themselves, and no control over their own minds. Their aggressive emotions are so powerful that they do not know what they are doing. They are actually crazy. Understanding this, we can learn to be compassionate.

Student: When I love someone a great deal, it is easy for that person to make me feel jealous. Why is this?
Rinpoche: Jealousy can occur only when there is fear or insecurity, some sense of weakness deep inside. When

you do not totally trust yourself, you may feel that the other person is taking advantage of you. But once you learn to trust your inner strength, there is nothing you can lose. Then you can discover how to love without making demands or creating jealousy.

Student: Buddhism doesn't seem to have the same attitude towards evil that other religions do.

Rinpoche: It would be foolish to say that bad actions are good, but without negativities to deal with, there would be no need for us to develop awareness, or meditation, or compassion. With no problems and negativities, we could not become enlightened; so we are fortunate in having both positive and negative situations to deal with. Although it is not easy to overcome our problems, they are our testing ground. Instead of being angry at those who harm us, we can be grateful to them for giving us the opportunity to develop patience—and even love and compassion. This way of seeing circumstances can further open our hearts.

Student: How can I develop a more compassionate heart?

Rinpoche: Work happily with other people and put as much energy into your heart as you can. Be natural and cheerful. Learn to accept others even with their faults. Although the highest positive feeling is called love, even love is bound by the subject-object relationship: we try to make those close to us conform to what we feel they should be. These may be our friends, our lovers, our children, or even God or Buddha. Only compassion frees us from this limiting relationship. Compassion accepts others as they are. One who thoroughly realizes compassion no longer sees any separation between 'self' and 'others'. Compassion is the wholesome and spontaneous response to all situations.

Student: It seems important to help other people out of compassion. Yet I don't often know what to do; I feel ignorant and helpless in most situations. Could you talk about that?

Rinpoche: The best way to show compassion is through wishing to help. When you cannot do anything about a situation, just wish sincerely that you could help. Although these are only thoughts, there is value in having good thoughts. You can also realize that the reason you cannot help is that you lack the wisdom and spiritual power to do so. But the wish will encourage you and give strength to your practice. The more you develop your practice, the more power you have to help others.

Wishing consists not of just words, but of a deep feeling which comes from the bottom of your heart. Once you have strongly developed this feeling, then willingness comes, and then openness. At this point you can act effectively. This is how compassion begins. You see others' problems, you feel their pain, their sorrow, their suffering. Your wishing to help becomes stronger as you open more, and feel more deeply.

Student: Sometimes it seems very selfish to say, "I can't do anything."

Rinpoche: Not when you really desperately want to help, but you know, realistically, that there is simply nothing you can do.

Student: I have many friends who are involved in the social movement, trying to change society. I, too, see many things that are wrong, but it is very hard to explain to someone else that meditation is going to help society. I get a lot of criticism that I don't know how to deal with, and yet I know that meditation is right.

Rinpoche: To help others, you must have both wisdom and power, which means compassion. When one or both of these qualities are lacking, it is difficult to succeed. Although you may have good intentions, lack of power means lack of effectiveness. It is better to develop your awareness, your power, and your ability to act.

First, you need to become sensitive to what a situation has in store; then you can deal with it in an appropriate way. Without preparation, good ideas are difficult to carry to completion.

Student: Wisdom and meditation sound very similar to me. What exactly is the connection?

Rinpoche: Yes, wisdom and meditation become very similar. Meditation is awareness; and when awareness is developed, then it becomes wisdom. When we understand the suffering of others, we can develop wishingness, then willingness, and then our hearts open. Wisdom allows us to see what can be done, and gives us the ability to alleviate others' sufferings.

The Seed of Enlightenment

Enlightenment is the nature of all experience, which means that enlightenment is available to us at all times. The self-image, however, cuts us off from the enlightened view—so most of us have little conviction that there is actually anything more to life than what we ordinarily experience. When we have these doubts, we may not even try to transcend the limitations our egos place on us. But when we see that there may be some truth in spiritual beliefs, we set out on a path that leads us beyond our limitations and to increasingly higher states of awareness. We become more and more awakened to our own nature, until finally there is nothing between us and the experience of enlightenment.

The teachings of the path to enlightenment have been passed on from teacher to student in an unbroken lineage reaching back to the Buddha himself. The Buddha taught, and those he taught in turn taught others.

This is the living tradition which maintains the path to enlightenment. Those who pass on the teachings do so by realizing the Buddha's teachings in themselves, and they therefore transmit not only the texts and their true meanings, but also the actual experience of enlightenment.

The masters of the lineage, working on inner levels, can transmit the enlightenment lineage directly—without words or concepts, without even the use of symbolic gestures or expressions. However, it is not easy to receive this transmission; our conceptual minds, our egos which judge and interpret all our experience, get in the way.

In what we usually call teaching, learning is a matter of filtering words and meanings through our conceptual understanding. But in the teachings of the path, because each word is a direct doorway to enlightenment, we need to understand the inner meanings by our direct experience. When our hearts and minds open to these deeper meanings, a teacher can then help us to transcend the limitations that our conceptual minds place on our understanding.

Both intellectual and experiential understanding grow and deepen together. Thus every step in the transmission—the teachings, the texts, and the learning process—must be carried out with utmost care, or the direct path to enlightenment will be obscured. Impatient with our progress, we may feel that the 'more' we learn the better off we are. But going from teacher to teacher diffuses our understanding instead of deepening it. We therefore need to carefully select an enlightened guide and then follow him until our understanding becomes deep and clear.

How can we be sure that our teacher will be able to guide us to this realization? With both our intelligence and our intuition as guides, we naturally are attracted to a teacher who has brought to completion those qualities we wish to develop in ourselves. A teacher lives the inner meaning of the teachings, and so we see in him our inner nature. Then, through his enlightened compassion, he helps us to develop our own qualities of compassion, integrity, and inner confidence.

When the teacher is compassionate and open, the path naturally unfolds, and our lives take on an even and flowing quality. Gradually we become more aware of our inner nature, and build up a depth of self-understanding and inner strength.

Yet the teachings do not always come in forms that are pleasing to us or to our egos. A compassionate teacher, in revealing our inner nature to our conscious awareness, also brings out those qualities that we do not like to admit in ourselves. We can get rid of these things once we see them, but these qualities may be such that our egos do not wish to give them up. And our egos, when they feel threatened with loss, may cause us to doubt the teachings and the teacher; they may even lead us to believe that if we do not like a certain teaching, it must certainly be wrong. At this point we may feel impelled to break with the teacher instead of our ego.

But to break with the teacher is to break with our trust in ourselves. By this picking and choosing, accepting and rejecting, we undercut our own development and strengthen only our limitations. In this way we not only invite confusion, but also a profound feeling of guilt and failure which makes further progress on the path extremely difficult.

Therefore, confidence in the teacher and in what he represents are needed from the start. For the lineage to continue unbroken, there must be mutual trust, openness, honesty, and integrity as the basis of the path. Communities built upon this foundation will continue to prosper, and the future of the lineage will be secure.

The teachings leading to direct experience are the touchstones for the stages of our growth. Finally, we discover that the teachings and our own experience of enlightenment have merged. We have transcended our samsaric nature. Now we see that all nature and all existence are already illumined.

Once we become enlightened, we become part of the lineage, and share the same living knowledge and understanding of the Buddha. This is the thread of enlightenment. We then carry this on in our own understanding, in our work in the world.

After this experience, no questions or doubts remain: we have understanding of the unbroken lineage. The inspiration of this ancient lineage of enlightenment lives within us, and we are open to the enlightenment nature that is inherent in all existence.

Index

of self-image, 14
of thoughts and images, 31
ground of being, 91ff, 129

healing, 47
health, 32
    effect of mind on, xii
Hinayana, xiii
honesty, 17ff, 48
human existence (importance
    of), 28, 30

illusion, 24, 70ff, 84, 104, 131
impermanence, 6, 29. *See also*
    transitoriness
inner balance, 44, 48, 63, 90
integration, 47, 117, 129

jealousy, 149
Jigmay Lingpa, 139

karma, 5, 6, 18, 21, 28, 75, 129.
    See also patterns

labelling (of experience), 23, 29,
    51, 74-75, 119
lineage, 152ff

Mahayana, xiii, 8
meanings, 62, 111ff
meditation, 30, 31ff, 55, 58, 79,
    81, 96ff, 112, 114, 128, 130,
    143, 151
    anxiety in, 66-67
    awareness in, 112, 151

experiential, 2ff, 128
exploring the senses in, 46
ground state in, 93
levels of, 93, 96
nature of the mind and, xii
penetrating fear in, 20, 23-24
relaxation and, 31ff, 55, 99
thoughts in, 103ff, 108
time with relationship to,
    36-37
transforming negative emo-
    tions in, 52ff, 57
transitoriness and, 73
wish for experiences in, 37-38
    66, 119-120
memories, 37, 41ff
middle path, 50, 64
mind, xii, 8, 47, 54, 66, 71, 80,
    91, 92, 93, 104, 105,
    121, 127
    meditation and the,
        79, 112-113
    nature of the, xii
    patterns of the, 40-41
mindfulness, 4, 36, 46, 118
    meditation and, 2
mystic experience, 37, 90

Nagarjuna, 130, 138
negativities, 42, 50, 51, 149
    transforming, 52ff, 62
nirvana, 5, 86, 92, 130, 131
Nyingma teachings, ix, xi, xii

openness, xiii, 46, 52, 63, 93, 105,
    110, 115, 119, 140, 147, 150

pain, 13, 28, 34, 52, 59-60
path, 31, 51, 141, 153
patience, 4, 54
patterns, 17ff, 40ff, 51, 66, 126.
    See also karma
  breaking, 18-19, 67
  of fear, 23
philosophy, 10, 80, 101, 102,
    111, 112
playfulness, 29, 55
pleasures, 44, 45
positive feelings, 47, 149
power, 137, 138, 150, 151
  of energy, 52

reality, 3, 11, 24, 70ff, 75, 76, 77,
    80ff, 96, 107, 119, 125, 126,
    129, 130
relative truth, 37, 72, 127
relaxation, 31, 41, 46ff, 56, 67,
    73, 87, 98, 115, 147
religion, 100
renunciation, 9
right action, 7, 8

samsara, 5, 6, 9, 85, 86, 92, 113,
    129, 131, 142
Sangha, 141ff
self-confidence, 44, 154
self-image, 12ff, 19-20, 75, 78,
    96, 152. *See also* ego
self-reliance, 43, 49
senses, 2, 44ff, 65, 93
  layers of, 46

society, 3, 10
space, 46, 90, 109, 110, 121, 128
  as ground level, 92
  of meditation, 97
spiritual path, 52, 63, 100,
    111-112
stress, xii, 32
subject-object orientation,
    12-13, 22-23, 34, 115, 117,
    119, 143, 149
suffering, 8, 10, 14, 52ff, 81-82,
    85-86, 115

teachers, 28, 100, 137, 152ff
thoughts, 23, 52, 53, 66-68, 79,
    88-89, 101, 103ff,
    120ff, 127
  awareness and, 96-97
  nature of, 104
  space between, 105ff, 121ff,
    129
  the watcher and, 120ff
Tibet, 76, 77
time, 3, 8, 9, 35-37, 53-54, 90,
    122, 127
transitoriness, 9, 27, 71. *See also*
    change
trust, 138, 139, 155
truth, 72, 96

Vajrayana, xii, xiii, xiv
visualizations, 130
  dream-lotus, 87ff

will, 4, 34

Other Dharma Publishing Books

Time, Space, and Knowledge: A New Vision of Reality by Tarthang Tulku. Thirty-five exercises and a rigorous philosophical text reveal new horizons of knowledge, unique in their richness and depth.

Kum Nye Relaxation by Tarthang Tulku. Exercises for discovering the relaxing energies within our bodies and senses.

Gesture of Balance by Tarthang Tulku. The Nyingma method of meditation wherein all life experience is meditation.

Skillful Means by Tarthang Tulku. A manual for making work a source of unlimited fulfillment.

Kindly Bent to Ease Us by Longchenpa. A translation of Longchenpa's guide to the Dzogchen path to enlightenment.

The Life and Liberation of Padmasambhava by Yeshe Tsogyal. A translation of the complete biography of Tibetan Buddhism's founder. Two volumes, 58 color plates.

Crystal Mirror Series edited by Tarthang Tulku. Introductory explorations of the various aspects of Tibetan philosophy, history, psychology, art, and culture. Five volumes currently available.

Calm and Clear by Lama Mipham. Translations of two beginning meditation texts by a brilliant 19th century Tibetan Lama.

If you order Dharma books directly from the publisher, it will help us to make more such books available. Write for a free catalog and new book announcements.

Dharma Publishing   2425 Hillside Avenue
Berkeley, California 94704   USA